EXPLORING THE WORLD OF GENERATIVE AI:

A Beginner's Guide to the Power and Potential of Artificial Intelligence, Implementing Generative AI in Your Business Processes for Increased Efficiency and Innovation.

Elio Scott

Copyright © 2025 Elio Scott

All rights reserved

The characters and events portrayed in this book are fictitious. Any similarity to real persons, living or dead, is coincidental and not intended by the author.

No part of this book may be reproduced, or stored in a retrieval system, or transmitted in any form or by any means, electronic, mechanical, photocopying, recording, or otherwise, without express written permission of the publisher.

Cover design by: Art Painter
Library of Congress Control Number: 2018675309
Printed in the United States of America

*I Want to thank you and congratulate you for buying my book
Exploring the World of Generative AI*

CONTENTS

Title Page

Copyright

Dedication

Introduction · 1

Chapter 1: Understanding Generative AI · 3

Chapter 2: Types Of Generative Models · 11

Chapter 3: Training And Evaluation · 42

Chapter 4: Generative AI For Business · 57

Chapter 5: Understanding Data Augmentation · 74

Chapter 6: Legal Document Generation · 87

Chapter 7: Overcoming Challenges And Risk · 102

Chapter 8: Marketing And Advertising · 128

Chapter 9 : Generative AI In Trading · 145

Chapter 10 : Generative AI And Machine Learning · 160

Conclusion · 173

May I Ask You For A Small Favor?

INTRODUCTION

Artificial Intelligence has become an integral part of our daily lives. As the world is moving towards automation and robotics From virtual assistants on our smartphones to self-driving cars, AI is everywhere. But there's more to AI than just what we see in science fiction movies or read about in news articles. One specific branch of AI that has been making headlines recently is Generative AI.

Generative AI is a subset of machine learning that focuses on creating systems that can generate new content, such as images, videos, music, or text. Unlike traditional machine learning algorithms that rely on pre-existing data to make predictions and decisions, generative AI systems are designed to come up with original ideas and creations without explicitly being programmed to do so. This ability to create something new makes generative AI a powerful tool for various industries, including art, music, gaming, and more.

◆ ◆ ◆

Hello, it's me, Elio Scott . Before you start reading my book I would like to ask you a favor: If you enjoy reading the book can you please leave an honest review for me in Amazon? - it will mean a lot to me! Thanks in advantage, and now be ready

ELIO SCOTT

to learn more about Generative AI :)

CHAPTER 1: UNDERSTANDING GENERATIVE AI

Generative AI systems work by analyzing large datasets and learning the patterns and features of the data to generate new content that is similar or related to the original data. This process is known as unsupervised learning, as the system learns from unlabelled data without any human intervention.

One of the main advantages of generative AI is its ability to create original content, which can be used for various purposes. For example, in the field of art, generative AI has been used to create unique and mesmerizing digital artworks that would have been impossible for humans to imagine or create.

Definition

Generative AI, also known as generative artificial intelligence or generative adversarial networks (GANs), is a subfield of artificial intelligence that deals with creating new content, such as images, videos, text, and even music.

It involves training algorithms to generate new data samples that are similar to the input data it was trained on. This process is achieved through a competition between two neural networks - a generator network and a discriminator network.

The generator creates new content that attempts to fool the discriminator, while the discriminator tries to correctly distinguish between real and generated data.

Historical Background

In the early days, Generative Adversarial Networks (GANs) were regarded as a major breakthrough in AI research. However, their origins can be traced back to the 1950s and 1960s.

During this time period, many scientists and researchers began exploring the idea of creating machines that could think and learn like humans. This led to the development of Artificial Intelligence (AI) as a field of study.

One of the earliest forms of generative AI was developed by mathematician and computer scientist, John von Neumann. In 1948, he proposed the concept of self-replicating machines that could improve themselves over time through learning and evolution. This idea laid the foundation for modern-day GANs.

In the 1950s, computer scientist and mathematician, Alan Turing, introduced the concept of "Turing Machines" which were theoretical computing machines that could simulate any algorithm or computation. This laid the groundwork for artificial neural networks (ANNs), which are a key component of GANs.

In 1965, renowned computer scientist and AI pioneer, Herbert Simon, wrote a book titled "The Shape of Automation: For Men and Management", where he discussed the idea of machines being able to generate new ideas and concepts. This concept of machine creativity would later become a fundamental aspect of GANs.

Fast forward to the 1990s, when scientist Ian Goodfellow proposed the initial framework for GANs as we know them today. However, it wasn't until 2014 when Goodfellow and his team released a paper detailing the mathematical framework for GANs that they gained widespread recognition.

Since then, GANs have been used in various applications such as image generation, text-to-image translation, and even music generation. They continue to be a hot topic of research and development in the field of Artificial Intelligence.

Moreover, the concept of Generative Adversarial Networks has also sparked ethical and societal debates. Some argue that GANs could potentially lead to a future where AI can create realistic fake images, videos, and even people, making it difficult to distinguish between what is real and what is not. This has raised concerns about privacy and security issues as well as the potential for misuse of GANs in creating fake news and propaganda.

On the other hand, proponents of GANs argue that they have immense potential in various industries such as entertainment, fashion, and design. GANs can be used to create new artistic styles and designs, generate realistic images for virtual reality applications, and even aid in drug discovery by generating molecule structures.

As GANs continue to improve and evolve, researchers and developers must consider the implications of this technology on society. Ethical guidelines and regulations must be in place to ensure responsible use of GANs and prevent any potential harm or misuse.

Fundamentals Of Generative Models

In recent years, we have seen immense growth in the field of Artificial Intelligence (AI) and Machine Learning. With advancements in technology and algorithms, AI has become a powerful tool for solving complex problems and generating valuable insights. One of the most fascinating areas of AI is Generative Modeling, which involves creating or synthesizing new data samples from existing ones.

Generative models are algorithms that learn how to generate new data samples by training on a dataset. These models use probability distributions and statistical methods to map the relationships between different data points in a given dataset. They are capable of generating high-quality outputs that resemble the original data and can be used for various applications, such as image generation, text-to-speech synthesis, and music composition.

Generative vs. Discriminative Models

Generative models and discriminative models are two different types of machine learning algorithms that serve different purposes. Both these models play a crucial role in the field of Generative AI, which is a subset of artificial intelligence focused on generating new data or content.

Generative Models: These models learn from existing data to create new data that follows the same distribution as the original dataset. Generative models are used to generate new content such as images, videos, text, or even music.

Discriminative Models: These models learn from existing data to classify or label new data based on the patterns they have learned from the training data. Discriminative models are commonly used for tasks like image recognition, speech recognition, and sentiment analysis.

Both these types of models have their own strengths and weaknesses, making them suitable for different applications. Generative models are more versatile as they can generate new data that is not limited to the existing dataset, while discriminative models are better at accurately classifying or predicting labels for new data.

Probability Theory In Generative Modeling

Generative AI is a rapidly advancing field that has shown immense potential in artificial intelligence research. One of the key areas in this field is generative modeling, which aims to create realistic data samples from a given distribution. In order to understand generative models better, it is important to have an understanding of probability theory.

Probability theory plays a crucial role in the development and evaluation of generative models. It provides the framework for understanding and quantifying uncertainty, which is a fundamental aspect of generative modeling. There are several key concepts from probability theory that are commonly used in generative models.

Probability Distributions

A probability distribution is a function that maps all possible outcomes of a random variable to their corresponding probabilities. In simpler terms, it describes the likelihood of each possible outcome occurring. In generative models, probability distributions are essential in representing the underlying data distribution.

Examples of commonly used probability distributions in generative modeling include

Gaussian (normal) distribution and Bernoulli distribution. These distributions are often used as building blocks for more complex generative models.

Bayesian Inference

Bayesian inference is a statistical method that allows us to update our beliefs about a system based on new evidence. In generative modeling, it is used to estimate the parameters of a probability distribution from observed data. Bayesian inference is particularly useful in situations where we have limited data and need to make predictions about unseen data points.

Bayesian Networks

A Bayesian network is a graphical representation of probabilistic relationships between variables. It consists of nodes, which represent random variables, and edges, which indicate the conditional dependencies between variables. Bayesian networks are commonly used in generative models as they provide an intuitive way to model complex systems and make predictions about unseen data.

Markov Chain Monte Carlo (MCMC)

Markov chain Monte Carlo (MCMC) is a class of algorithms that are used to approximate complex probability distributions. It involves sampling from a Markov chain to generate a sequence of samples that converge to the desired distribution. MCMC is commonly used in generative modeling for parameter estimation and model selection.

Variational Inference

Variational inference is another approach for approximating complex probability distributions. It involves approximating the target distribution with a simpler one, such as a Gaussian distribution, using optimization techniques. Variational inference is often used in generative models for its computational efficiency and scalability.

Deep Generative Models

Deep generative models are a class of generative models that use deep neural networks to learn complex relationships between variables. They have gained popularity in recent years due to their ability to generate high-quality samples and model complex data distributions. Some examples of popular deep generative models include variational autoencoders, generative adversarial networks, and autoregressive models.

CHAPTER 2: TYPES OF GENERATIVE MODELS

Types Of Generative Models

1. Autoencoders

The core principle of an autoencoder is learning to perfect an identity function under some form of reconstruction error. It's a type of unsupervised learning, which means the input data isn't labeled. Instead, the network is trained to encode the input into a minimal representation (encoded state) and then decode it back to its original form with as few errors as possible.

Here's a simple breakdown:

1. **Encoder Network:** This initial stage compresses the input data into a latent space representation. It's akin to a funnel, taking the raw data and squeezing it into a lower-dimensional form.
2. **Decoder Network:** The second part of the autoencoder then reconstructs the encoded data back into its original format as closely as it can. These networks can be simple or highly complex, depending on the application.

The optimization of the network is achieved through backpropagation, constantly tweaking the weights to minimize the difference between the input and the output. This 'reconstruction error' drives the autoencoder to learn meaningful representations of the data.

Applications Of Autoencoders

Autoencoders have gained popularity due to their versatility and ability to handle a variety of data types. Here's how they are transforming different sectors:

Image And Video Processing

In image processing, autoencoders are used to reduce the size of large image files without losing key information. This makes them essential in applications ranging from satellite imagery to healthcare, where large amounts of data need to be stored or transmitted efficiently. They can also be used in denoising images, where the network learns to produce a clean image from a noisy one by focusing on the most essential parts.

Anomaly Detection

Autoencoders can learn the 'normal' state of a system by being exposed to a large volume of non-anomalous data. Once trained, they should be able to reconstruct 'normal' data quite well. Here, if an autoencoder encounters an anomaly, the reconstruction error will be significantly higher, alerting the system that something might be wrong. This is invaluable in fraud detection, cyber security, and even predictive maintenance in machinery.

Data Compression

By learning to represent the data in a compressed form, autoencoders offer a means of data reduction. This is crucial in fields where data size is a major constraint, such as in IoT devices or in storing large datasets.

Benefits Of Autoencoders

The versatility of autoencoders brings with it a host of benefits to the data scientist's toolkit.

Improved Data Representation

Autoencoders can learn complex patterns within the data, often outperforming traditional feature extraction methods. They can capture the nuanced relationships between various features, leading to richer representations that can be more highly correlated with the intended use of the data.

Enhanced Data Reconstruction

The very principle of an autoencoder, optimized to minimize the reconstruction error, means it can be highly efficient at reconstructing and denoising data, providing cleaner and more organized datasets that can improve the performance of a range of machine learning algorithms.

Efficient Feature Learning

Autoencoders have the ability to automatically learn features from the data, which can lead to more efficient and streamlined machine-learning pipelines. This can be particularly useful when the data is high-dimensional and there's a need to reduce the feature set while retaining essential information.

Challenges And Limitations

Autoencoders are not without their hurdles, and understanding their limitations is crucial in their practical application.

Training Complexity

Training an autoencoder can be a time-consuming process, especially for larger, more complex networks, which require a significant amount of data and computational resources. This is a barrier, particularly for smaller organizations or individuals with limited access to such resources.

Overfitting Issues

There's a risk of overfitting, where the model becomes too specific to the training data and doesn't generalize well to new data. Techniques such as dropout and regularization can mitigate this risk, but they add another layer of complexity to an already intricate network.

Interpretability Concerns

For many applications, such as in healthcare or

legal domains, being able to explain the decisions made by a model is just as important as the performance metrics. Autoencoders, like most deep learning models, can be opaque in their decision-making process, which can be a barrier to their adoption.

Real-World Examples

Industry Applications of Autoencoders

In the financial industry, autoencoders are used for fraud detection. By learning to reconstruct a client's typical financial behavior, the model can detect any unusual transactions that could indicate fraudulent activities.

In the e-commerce sector, autoencoders are used to power recommendation systems. By learning the underlying patterns in customer purchase data, the model can efficiently recommend products based on a customer's preferences.

In the manufacturing sector, autoencoders play a crucial role in predictive maintenance. By learning the 'healthy' behavior of machines, the model can detect anomalies and predict failures before they happen, saving on costly downtime and repairs.

2. Demystifying Variational Autoencoders (VAEs)

VAEs belong to the autoencoder family, a class of artificial neural networks employing unsupervised learning to encode inputs into a hidden, or latent, space representation. But VAEs go beyond mere data compression—they're a revolutionary approach to generative modeling.

Explaining VAEs In Simple Terms

Imagine a black box that can take any input, such as an image, and convert it into a simplified representation, capturing its core features. Then, this box can take that simplified version and 'decode' it back into an image that resembles the original input. This is essentially what a VAE does. It learns the probabilistic distribution of the data, meaning it can also generate new outputs similar to the ones it's been trained on.

Applications In Image Generation, Data Compression And Anomaly Detection

The capability of VAEs to represent complex data efficiently has immense implications. In the visual arts, VAEs can create hyperrealistic images, while in anomaly detection, they can pinpoint deviations in the data that lie outside what's considered 'normal.' Furthermore, VAEs in tandem with other AI systems can even enhance the compression of large data files without loss of information—a critical feature in fields where storage and data transfer are constraints.

How VAEs Work

To appreciate the workings of VAEs, one must understand their core architecture and the concept of the latent space, which forms the bedrock of their operations.

Encoder-Decoder Architecture

At their heart, VAEs consist of an encoder network that compresses the input data into a latent space and a decoder network that maps points in the latent space back to the original space. Both the encoder and decoder use a combination of probabilistic and deterministic approaches, with the encoder acting as a recognition network that learns the parameters of the distribution in the latent space, and the decoder as a generative network that samples from this latent representation.

Latent Space Representation

The latent space is the conceptual space in which data is transformed and consistently represented in a reduced dimensionality. It's this latent space that gives VAEs their generative power—the ability to produce novel outputs that are variations of the ones they have learned in training. By sampling from the latent space, the model can synthesize data points that share the same distribution as the training data.

Benefits Of VAEs

VAEs offer multiple advantages over traditional

autoencoders, particularly in terms of data representation and generation.

Improved Data Representation

The latent space representation learned by the VAE can provide a deeper and more meaningful representation of the input data. In image recognition, for example, this means that the VAE can identify characteristics of images in a way that is less sensitive to noise and other perturbations.

Enhanced Data Generation Capabilities

The generative nature of VAEs allows them to create data points that are novel yet share similar properties to the original dataset. This is particularly powerful in applications where large volumes of data synthesis are required, such as in the training of other machine learning models on augmented datasets.

Challenges And Limitations

While VAEs offer immense potential, they are not without their challenges. Understanding and working with VAEs can be complex, and there are limitations to their capabilities, particularly in terms of interpretability and training.

Training Complexity

The training process for VAEs can be more intricate than for standard autoencoders due to their probabilistic nature. This requires careful consideration of the loss function, which balances both the reconstruction error and the learned distribution of the latent space.

Latent Space Interpretability

One of the main drawbacks of VAEs is the interpretability of the latent space. Unlike traditional autoencoders, the representations in the latent space do not necessarily correspond to easily interpretable features, which can make it difficult to understand how the model is making its decisions.

Real-World Examples

Despite the complexity and challenges, VAEs have made significant inroads in a multitude of real-world applications, showcasing their power and versatility.

Illustrative Applications In Diverse Fields

In the realm of healthcare, VAEs have been used to generate synthetic medical images, aiding in the training of AI systems without risking patient data. In fashion and design, VAEs can assist in creating new and unique styles based on learning from vast image databases. Even in the financial sector, VAEs can detect anomalous patterns in financial transactions and market data, safeguarding against fraud and market manipulation.

VAEs represent a marvel of modern technology, pushing the boundaries of what is possible in generative modeling and data representation. While they may seem enigmatic at first glance, VAEs are grounded in sound theoretical principles that enable them to reshape our understanding of artificial intelligence and its potential applications for the betterment of our world. Whether it's through the lens of artistic creation, data compression, or anomaly detection, the influence of VAEs is set to permeate various spheres of human endeavor, leaving an indelible mark on the future of technology.

3. Generative Adversarial Networks (GANs)

Generative Adversarial Networks, or GANs, are a class of machine learning frameworks that employ two neural networks, pitting one against the other to generate new, synthetic instances of data that can pass for real data. They were first introduced by Ian Goodfellow and his colleagues in 2014 and have since sparked a revolution in the field of artificial intelligence.

Definition And Mechanics

At its core, GANs harness a competitive dynamic to produce complex, realistic-looking images, sounds, and other data types. One network, known as the "Generator," creates new realistic-looking data instances, while the other, the "Discriminator," evaluates them to determine if they're real or fake. Through a continual feedback loop, the Generator learns to produce data that are indistinguishable from the authentic samples, and the Discriminator becomes adept at differentiating between the two. The back-and-forth competition forces both networks to improve progressively until the Generator creates data that is, to human observers, virtually indistinguishable from the real thing.

Real-World Applications And Daily Impact

While the technicalities of GANs can be daunting, their real-world applications are more relatable than you might think. GANs are responsible for shaping the pictures we post, the movies we watch, and even the clothes we wear.

The most famous application of GANs is in Deepfakes, a technology known to the public for its infamous ability to superimpose one person's face onto another person's body convincingly in video footage. However, GANs also have a wide range of other applications such as image-to-image translation (e.g., changing a painted scene into a photo-realistic picture or vice versa), generating high-resolution images from low-resolution ones, and even filling in the gaps in pictures where data is incomplete.

Benefits Of GANs

Beyond their early infamy, GANs hold a trove of valuable uses that have the potential to positively impact our lives. Here are a few ways they are already doing so.

Personalization In Online Experiences

One of the most profound effects of GANs could be the personalization of our online world to an unprecedented degree. By understanding our preferences, GANs can craft an individualized internet experience through customized shopping suggestions, tailored news feeds, and personalized product designs.

Enhancing Creativity And Art

Artists and creatives are exploring GANs to push the boundaries of their craft. From producing unique visual art to generating music and literature, GAN-based AI is unlocking new realms of creative expression, often leading to collaborations between humans and machines.

Improving Data Security And Privacy

Strikingly, GANs are also our allies in the fight for data security and privacy. By predicting potential weaknesses in cybersecurity systems, GANs help developers stay one step ahead in the never-ending battle against cyber threats.

Challenges And Misconceptions

It wouldn't be an AI without stirring up a healthy dose of debate and skepticism. Ethical quandaries and misconceptions are part and parcel of GAN technology.

Ethical Concerns And Risks

With GANs, the line between reality and artificiality has never been blurrier. Deepfake technology, while astounding, raises serious ethical concerns. Misuse of GANs can undermine data integrity, lead to misinformation, and potentially influence crucial societal decisions.

Common Misconceptions About GANs

A common misperception is that GANs represent the pinnacle of AI's capabilities. In reality, they are a single thread in the rich tapestry of AI development, powerful but not all-encompassing. Another misconception is that they somehow operate autonomously, overlooking the fact that human oversight and intervention are always critical.

Future Implications

The GAN revolution is just getting started, and its potential seems boundless. Here's how GANs might further embed themselves in our future.

GANs In Upcoming Technologies And Everyday Products

We can expect to see GANs play a significant role in developing new products and experiences by correctly predicting consumer trends, creating lifelike virtual models for online catalogs, and continually refining themselves through the constant influx of user data.

Potential Evolution And Impact On Society

The evolution of GANs has the potential to fundamentally transform society, serving as the bedrock for the next generation of technological advancements. Nonetheless, we'll witness continuous debates on their moral usage and necessity in our daily routine, challenging us to recalibrate our understanding of authenticity and consent in an AI-saturated world.

Indeed, GANs embody the creative rebellion within AI, advocating for the unbounded possibilities of synthetic data. They stand not as solitary disruptors but rather as pioneers in a larger conversation about the role of AI innovations in contemporary life. Whether as artists, analysts, or guardians of our digital integrity, GANs have proved they are more than an arcane tool in the tech world — they are the covert architects of our digital future.

4. Flow-Based Models

Flow-based models belong to the family of generative models within AI. Unlike traditional discriminative models that differentiate between classes of data, generative models create new data instances. They achieve this by learning the true probability distribution underlying the dataset, which allows them to generate samples that are statistically similar to the training data. Flow-based models are unique in how they approach this task, using invertible neural networks to map a simple distribution (e.g., normal distribution) to the true data space, allowing for efficient and iterative generation of new instances.

Flow-Based Models At Work

These models have a remarkable ability to capture complex dependencies in the data, often yielding samples that are more diverse and of higher quality than other generative models. They have seen successes in fields like image generation, text-to-speech synthesis, molecular design, and even reinforcement learning. Their versatility makes them attractive tools for various sectors from entertainment to healthcare.

Advantages Of Flow-Based Models

In comparison to other generative AI models, flow-based models offer unique benefits that have significant implications for businesses and society.

High-Quality Sample Generation

The flow-based approach often results in generating data that is less prone to artifacts and more diverse than that produced by traditional models. This high-dimensional sample generation is invaluable in applications requiring realistic, varied data production.

Scalability and Efficiency

Flow-based models possess inherent parallelizability, which translates to improved scalability on modern computing architectures like GPUs and TPUs. This, coupled with their efficiency in training, makes flow-based models an alluring prospect for tasks that demand rapid, large-scale generation.

Data Privacy And Security Benefits

The invertible transformations within flow-based models provide a unique benefit for data privacy and security. Due to their ability to revert to the original training samples, these models can generate synthetic data for analysis without risk of exposure or violation of data security protocols.

Challenges And Limitations

While the benefits are substantial, flow-based models are not without their hurdles. These challenges need to be addressed for wider and more effective implementation.

Training Complexity

Flow-based models often require complex training procedures, especially when dealing with high-dimensional or multi-modal data. Achieving convergence in these scenarios can be computationally intensive and time-consuming.

Handling High-Dimensional Data

The modeling of high-dimensional spaces is an area where flow-based models face difficulties. The curse of dimensionality can lead to inefficiencies in training and may require innovative solutions to achieve optimal performance.

Interpretability Concerns

Interpretability is a key concern in the realm of AI, and flow-based models, with their complex transformations, can be opaque in explaining the reasoning behind their outputs. This is a critical limitation, particularly in applications with regulatory, ethical, or interpretive requirements.

Real-World Examples

To appreciate the significance of flow-based models, it's crucial to look at their real-world applications where they are proving their mettle.

Showcase Industries Benefiting From Flow-Based Models

Some of the industries harnessing flow-based models include:

1. **Healthcare:** For synthesizing medical images, drug discovery, and patient data generation.
2. **Finance:** In risk assessment simulation and stock market analysis.
3. **Creativity and Design:** For creating art, music, and innovative product designs.

Case Studies Demonstrating Successful Implementations

1. **Healthcare Imaging:** A notable case saw flow-based models used to generate high-

quality synthetic images for pathology analysis, which significantly improved the training and validation of image-based models, particularly in cancer detection.
2. **Financial Risk Simulation:** Flow-based models have been implemented to create synthetic portfolio data for scenario analysis, allowing for improved risk management and more accurate prediction.
3. **Text Generation:** In the domain of natural language processing, flow-based models have been pivotal in generating coherent and contextually relevant text, advancing automated content generation and chatbot capabilities.

5. Autoregressive Models

Autoregressive models are a subset of generative models that learn the probability distribution of data they were trained on. They work by recounting data points in a sequence, where each data point's choice is influenced by preceding data points. In essence, they 'remember' past decisions to inform future ones, which is pivotal for text and sequential pattern generation, where order is critical.

The technical mechanics involve the use of recurring neural networks (RNNs), typically long short-term memory (LSTM) units or

Gated Recurrent Units (GRUs). These networks have temporal 'memory' and can pinpoint dependencies over large swathes of input. This means autocorrelation rather than external influences guides the model's generative process.

Applications In Daily Life

The reach of autoregressive models, fuelled by deep learning technology, extends into our lives in ways that are both subtle and pervasive. From predicting our next word when typing a message to creating novel pieces of art, these models quietly orchestrate the symphony of our digital lives.

Image Generation

One of the most prominent applications has been in image generation. Models like PixelRNN and PixelCNN create pictures one pixel at a time, with each new pixel's color determined by the ones generated before it. This has led to the creation of entirely synthetic images, some so detailed that they're mistaken for photographs.

Text Prediction

Autoregressive models sit at the heart of modern language models such as GPT-3, capable of astonishing feats in natural language processing. They anticipate what word comes next in a sentence or what the next line of a verse might be, based on the context of what came before it.

Voice Synthesis

Voice synthesis models like WaveNet have leveraged autoregression to produce speech where each sound is carefully calculated based on the phonetic context, allowing for a more realistic and natural-sounding voice.

Benefits

The deployment of autoregressive models brings a wealth of benefits, which are not just limited to the accuracy of predictions, but also extend to personalization and efficiency in daily tasks.

Personalization In Services

Companies can leverage autoregressive models to offer highly personalized recommendations, predictions, and content based on individual user behavior and history. This personal touch enhances user engagement and satisfaction.

Enhanced User Experiences

Autoregressive models power AI chatbots and assistants, improving customer service by predicting and responding to user inquiries with a degree of human-like comprehension and nuance.

Time-saving Applications

In applications such as automatic code completion, these models can save time and reduce the cognitive load by predicting the next lines of code, applying the principle of write less, produce more.

Challenges And Limitations

However, no advancement in AI comes without caveats. Autoregressive models, like all AI systems, are not immune to challenges and limitations, some of which are profound and require considered addresses.

Data Privacy Concerns

The very premise of autoregressive models—deep analysis and data retention—can be at odds with privacy expectations. The collection and use of massive datasets for training, often including sensitive personal information, must be monitored and controlled.

Bias In Generated Content

AI models, if trained on biased datasets, can perpetuate and sometimes exacerbate societal biases. This has often manifested in language models that reflect or reproduce racial, gender, and cultural stereotypes—raising ethical concerns that need to be addressed.

Computational Requirements

Training autoregressive models demand colossal computational resources, from energy-intensive data center servers to specialized hardware accelerators such as GPUs and TPUs. This poses barriers for smaller organizations and researchers.

Future Implications

Looking ahead, the integration of autoregressive AI into our daily technologies is inevitable. From smartphones to household appliances, we will interact with AI-generated content more frequently than we realize. What's important is to shape this future in a way that maintains the equilibrium between technological advancement and societal well-being.

Integration Into Everyday Technologies

The continued refinement of autoregressive models will see their integration into everyday consumer technologies, enhancing personalization and user experience across the board.

Ethical Considerations And Regulations

To ensure the responsible use of autoregressive AI, there is an urgent need for ethical guidelines and robust regulatory frameworks. Transparency in AI development and operation, along with stakeholder collaboration, will be crucial.

Applications Of Generative AI

One of the most well-known applications of generative AI is in the field of art and design. With generative AI, artists and designers can create unique and captivating pieces that were previously unimaginable. This technology allows for the exploration of new creative possibilities, pushing the boundaries of traditional art forms.

Image Generation

One of the most popular applications of generative AI is image generation. Generative adversarial networks (GANs) have gained a lot of attention in recent years due to their ability to generate realistic images that are indistinguishable from real images. GANs work by training two neural networks, one called the generator and the other called the discriminator.

The generator network takes in random noise as input and generates images, while the discriminator network tries to differentiate between real and fake images. Through a process of constant back-and-forth competition, the generator network learns to create increasingly realistic images.

Text Generation

Another popular application of generative AI is text generation. Natural language processing (NLP) techniques combined with deep learning have enabled computers to generate human-like text. This is achieved through recurrent neural networks (RNNs), which are trained on large datasets of text.

One use case for text generation is in chatbots, where the AI can generate responses and hold conversations with users. This technology has been leveraged in customer service, where chatbots can handle simple queries and free up human agents to focus on more complex tasks.

Text generation has also been used in content creation, with AI writing articles and reports based on data inputs. This can be useful for generating reports that require repetitive writing or summarizing large amounts of data.

In the future, text generation through generative AI could potentially be used in language translation and even creative writing. As technology advances, it will become even more difficult to distinguish between human-written and AI-generated text. This raises ethical concerns, such as plagiarism and authenticity of written works. So while generative AI has many potential applications, it is important to consider the implications and use it responsibly.

Music Generation

Generative AI has also made advancements in the field of music generation. Through deep learning algorithms, AI can analyze and learn from existing musical compositions to create original pieces.

One notable use case for music generation is in film and video game soundtracks. Instead of hiring composers or using pre-made stock music, AI can generate unique and fitting soundscapes for different scenes or levels. This can save time and resources for production companies, while also offering a high level of customization.

Additionally, the music generation has the potential to revolutionize the music industry. AI can help composers and musicians generate ideas and melodies, serving as a tool for inspiration. It could also aid in creating personalized soundtracks for individual listeners, based on their preferences and mood.

Art And Design

Generative AI has made a significant impact in the fields of art and design. It allows artists and designers to push the boundaries of their creativity by using algorithms to generate unique and original content.

One notable application of generative AI in art is its use in creating digital paintings. By analyzing a large dataset of images, generative AI algorithms can learn to paint like famous artists or create entirely new styles and techniques. This has opened up new possibilities for digital artists, who can now use these algorithms as tools to enhance their own work or even as a medium for creating art.

Data Augmentation

In the realm of machine learning and artificial intelligence, data augmentation plays a pivotal role by expanding the diversity of data available for training models, without actually collecting new data. This is particularly valuable in scenarios where acquiring additional real-world data is costly or infeasible. Generative AI significantly contributes to this field by generating synthetic data that mimics real data sets. This approach allows for the enhancement of model accuracy and robustness by exposing the model to a broader variety of data scenarios, thereby reducing overfitting and improving the model's ability to generalize to new, unseen data.

Video Games

Generative AI is revolutionizing the video game industry by offering possibilities that were once deemed science fiction. Game developers are leveraging these technologies to create more dynamic, engaging, and unpredictable gaming environments. Through the use of generative AI, elements such as landscapes, characters, and even plotlines can be procedurally generated, offering a unique experience to every player. This not only enhances the replayability of games but also enables developers to craft vast, intricate worlds with significantly less manual effort. Furthermore, generative AI can adapt game difficulty in real-time, personalizing the gaming experience to match the skill level of individual players, thus keeping engagement high and frustration low.

Drug Discovery

In the pharmaceutical industry, generative AI is emerging as a game-changer in the field of drug discovery. By leveraging complex algorithms, it has the potential to predict how different chemical compounds will interact with biological targets, thereby speeding up the drug development process. This innovative approach can significantly reduce the time and financial investment required to bring new medications to market. Furthermore, generative AI can uncover novel compounds with therapeutic potential that might not have been identified through traditional research methods. This accelerates the path to finding effective treatments for a myriad of diseases, ultimately contributing to advancements in healthcare and medicine.

Chatbots And Virtual Assistants

Generative AI is revolutionizing the way businesses interact with customers through the development of sophisticated chatbots and virtual assistants. These AI-driven tools can understand and process natural language, enabling them to communicate with users in a way that feels personal and human-like. By analyzing vast amounts of data, they can provide accurate responses, offer recommendations, and even predict customer needs before they arise. This not only improves customer service efficiency but also enhances user satisfaction by providing instant support and personalized interactions.

Furthermore, as these technologies continue to evolve, chatbots and virtual assistants are expected to become even more integrated into daily business operations, streamlining processes and facilitating a more seamless customer experience.

Fashion Design

Generative AI is also making significant strides in the domain of fashion design, transforming traditional methods and introducing an innovative approach to creating apparel. By analyzing trends, patterns, and historical data, AI algorithms can generate unique design concepts that push the boundaries of creativity and style. This not only accelerates the design process but also enables designers to explore an extensive array of possibilities that were previously unimaginable. Additionally, AI-driven tools can customize designs based on individual preferences and body shapes, offering a personalized shopping experience that enhances customer satisfaction. With the integration of generative AI, the fashion industry is poised for a revolution, where technology and creativity converge to redefine trends and redefine what is possible in fashion design.

Speech Synthesis

The strides in speech synthesis technology have been monumental, providing an experience that's closer than ever to human conversation. This technology, often embodied through voice assistants and text-to-speech applications, leverages deep learning techniques to produce natural-sounding speech that includes intonations, emotions, and pauses found in daily human interactions. Beyond mere voice generation, current developments aim at understanding context and adjusting tone accordingly, making interactions with machines more intuitive and life-like. This progression not only enriches user experience but also opens new avenues for accessibility, allowing those with visual impairments or reading difficulties to engage with digital content more effectively. With ongoing advancements, the potential applications for speech synthesis are boundless, extending from personalized virtual assistants to more immersive storytelling and educational tools, thereby augmenting our interaction with technology.

Predictive Modeling

Predictive modeling has emerged as a key technology, harnessing the power of machine learning and data analysis to forecast future events with significant accuracy. This technology processes historical data to identify patterns and predict outcomes, playing a crucial role in various industries from finance to healthcare. In finance, it aids in identifying market trends and forecasting stock performances. Meanwhile, in healthcare, predictive models can anticipate disease outbreaks or patient readmissions, enabling proactive measures. The ability of predictive modeling to process vast amounts of data and learn from it makes it invaluable for decision-making processes, risk management, and strategic planning. Its continuous evolution promises even greater accuracy and applications, potentially transforming how we anticipate and respond to future challenges.

Personalization

Personalization stands as a pivotal advancement within technology, tailor-fitting experiences, and interactions to meet individual preferences and needs. Leveraging data analytics and artificial intelligence, it allows for customization that was once thought to be unattainable, from personalized shopping recommendations on e-commerce platforms to content feeds on social media uniquely curated for each user. In the realm of education, personalization transforms learning by adapting the pace and style to suit each student's learning habits, thereby improving engagement and outcomes. Beyond enhancing user experience, personalization also holds significant potential in healthcare by enabling treatments and health plans specifically designed for an individual's genetic makeup and lifestyle, marking a shift towards more predictive and preventive care.

Data Generation

Data Generation is emerging as a frontier in technological advancements, pivotal for the development and enhancement of machine learning models and artificial intelligence systems. Through techniques like synthetic data generation and augmentation, it becomes possible to create vast, diverse datasets without compromising privacy or ethical standards. This innovation is crucial, especially in fields where real-world data can be scarce or sensitive, such as in healthcare for rare diseases or in autonomous vehicle testing. By generating high-quality, realistic data, developers and researchers can train models more effectively and efficiently, accelerating progress and innovation. In essence, Data Generation not only addresses the challenges of data scarcity and privacy concerns but also opens new pathways for exploring complex scenarios and improving predictive dynamics in technology-driven solutions.

CHAPTER 3: TRAINING AND EVALUATION

Training a generative AI model requires large amounts of data and computing power. This is because the model needs to learn patterns and relationships within the data in order to generate meaningful outputs. The training process involves feeding the model with a vast amount of data and adjusting its parameters until it can accurately generate new content.

Data Preparation

Data preparation is an essential step in training a generative AI model. The data used to train the model should be relevant and diverse, covering a wide range of examples and scenarios. This helps the model to learn patterns and relationships from different perspectives, resulting in better output generation.

Data Collection And Preprocessing

Data collection is the first step in data preparation and involves gathering a large dataset of relevant information. This can include text, images, audio, or any other form of data that the model is expected to generate. The quality and quantity of the data have a direct impact on the performance of the generative AI model.

Once the data is collected, it needs to be

preprocessed before being fed into the model for training. This includes tasks such as cleaning, formatting, and normalizing the data to ensure consistency and accuracy.

Choice Of Generative Model

Generative models are a popular approach to creating artificial intelligence systems that can generate new data, based on the patterns and trends in the existing dataset. These models learn from the data and then generate new samples that are similar to the training data. Generative AI has been successfully applied in various fields such as image generation, text generation, music composition, and even video game design.

There are different types of generative models, each with its own strengths and weaknesses. Choosing the right model for a particular task is crucial in achieving good performance and accurate results. Some of the popular generative models include Variational Autoencoders (VAEs), Generative Adversarial Networks (GANs), and Autoregressive Models.

Architecture Design

The architecture design for generative AI models is crucial to the overall performance and functionality of the model. It involves deciding on the specific type of neural network, its structure, and the training process.

There are two main types of generative AI models: autoregressive models and GANs (Generative Adversarial Networks). Autoregressive models use sequential data to generate outputs, while GANs use two competing neural networks to generate realistic data.

In terms of structure, generative AI models can be designed with various layers and techniques such as convolutional layers for image generation or recurrent layers for sequential data. The specific architecture design depends on the type of data the model will be trained on and the desired output.

Lastly, the training process is a crucial aspect of architecture design. The model needs to be trained on a large dataset to capture the underlying patterns and generate accurate outputs. It also involves fine-tuning the hyperparameters of the model, such as learning rate and batch size, to optimize its performance.

Hyperparameter Tuning

Hyperparameter tuning is an essential step in training and evaluating a generative AI model. As the name suggests, hyperparameters are parameters whose values affect the behavior of the model during training. Examples of hyperparameters include learning rate, batch size, number of layers, and activation functions.

Choosing appropriate values for these hyperparameters can greatly impact the performance and accuracy of a generative AI model. However, finding the optimal values can be a challenging and time-consuming task.

One common approach to hyperparameter tuning is grid search, where different combinations of values for each hyperparameter are tested and evaluated. This method can be effective but can also take a significant amount of time, especially when dealing with large datasets and complex models.

Another popular technique for hyperparameter tuning is random search, where values for each hyperparameter are randomly selected and evaluated. This method can be more efficient than grid search, as it allows for a wider range of values to be explored.

In recent years, there has been a growing interest in using automated methods for hyperparameter tuning, such as Bayesian optimization and genetic algorithms. These techniques use machine learning algorithms to automatically search for the optimal values of hyperparameters, based on past evaluations and a predefined objective function.

Grid Search

Grid Search stands as a pivotal technique in the

domain of hyperparameter optimization, offering a structured method to meticulously explore the potential space of hyperparameter values. By defining a grid of hyperparameter values, it systematically trains and evaluates a model for each combination of parameters, ensuring that no stone is left unturned in the quest for the ideal configuration. Although Grid Search is celebrated for its thoroughness, it's important to acknowledge its scalability challenges, particularly with models that necessitate a substantial computation budget or when dealing with an extensive range of hyperparameters. Despite these constraints, its simplicity and the completeness of its search make it a valuable tool in the initial stages of model tuning, especially when used in conjunction with more efficient methods to fine-tune promising configurations.

Random Search

Random Search, contrasting with Grid Search's structured approach, introduces a level of stochasticity and flexibility that can be highly beneficial in the hyperparameter optimization process. Instead of evaluating every possible combination of parameters within a predefined grid, Random Search randomly selects combinations within the specified hyperparameter space. This method can significantly reduce the computational burden, especially in scenarios where the hyperparameter space is vast and the optimal solution resides in a less anticipated region. By not restricting the exploration to a finite grid, Random Search has the potential to discover effective solutions with fewer iterations. Its efficiency makes it particularly appealing for preliminary exploration and in cases where computational resources are limited. While it may not guarantee the thoroughness of Grid Search, Random Search offers a pragmatic balance between the breadth of search and computational feasibility, often leading to sufficiently optimal solutions within a shorter timeframe.

Bayesian Optimization

Bayesian Optimization stands out as a probabilistic model-based optimization technique designed for the optimization of black-box functions that are expensive to evaluate. It operates by building a probabilistic model of the objective function and uses it to select the most promising parameters to evaluate in the true objective function. This approach is particularly effective in fine-tuning hyperparameters of machine learning models where each evaluation can be time-consuming and resource-intensive. Bayesian Optimization iteratively updates its model based on the outcomes of previous evaluations, thus learning to focus its search on regions of the parameter space that are likely to yield the best performance. Its strength lies in its ability to balance exploration of the parameter space with exploitation of the known promising areas, making it highly efficient, especially in situations with a limited budget for function evaluations. While more complex than Grid Search and Random Search, Bayesian Optimization's intelligent search strategy can lead to superior results with fewer function evaluations, making it an invaluable tool in the optimization of machine learning algorithms.

Training Strategies

Training strategies play a crucial role in the success of generative AI models. These strategies involve techniques and methods used to train and optimize models for better performance.

One common training strategy is reinforcement learning, which involves an agent interacting with its environment and trying different actions to maximize a reward signal. This approach has been successfully applied to tasks such as language translation, image generation, and game-playing.

Another popular training strategy is generative adversarial networks (GANs), which involve two neural networks competing against each other. One network, known as the generator, creates new samples that resemble the training data, while the other network, called the discriminator, tries to identify whether the sample is real or fake. This approach has shown impressive results in generating realistic images and videos.

Transfer learning is also a commonly used training strategy in generative AI, where a pre-trained model is fine-tuned on a new dataset to perform a specific task. This allows models to leverage knowledge from previous tasks and reduces the need for large amounts of data.

Different training strategies may work better for different types of generative AI models and tasks. It is essential to carefully consider the characteristics of the data and the desired outcome when choosing a training strategy.

Evaluation Metrics

Evaluating generative AI models is a challenging task due to their inherent complexity and lack of ground truth. However, several metrics have been developed to assess the performance of these models objectively.

One common metric used in generative AI is perplexity, which measures how well a model predicts the next token in a sequence. Lower perplexity indicates better performance.

Another commonly used metric is the Inception Score, which evaluates the quality and diversity of generated images by comparing them to real images. A higher Inception Score reflects better diversity and realism in generated samples.

Some other evaluation metrics include Fréchet Inception Distance (FID), which measures how similar generated samples are to real data in terms of statistics, and Kernel Inception Distance (KID), which compares the features learned by a generative model with those learned from real data.

It is important to understand the strengths and limitations of different evaluation metrics and choose the most appropriate one for a specific model and task. Additionally, it is essential to continuously improve and develop new evaluation metrics that better reflect the performance of generative AI models.

Techniques For Stabilizing Training

Neural networks, and specifically deep learning models, have shown great promise in generative artificial intelligence tasks. These models can learn complex patterns and generate high-quality outputs with little or no human intervention. However, training these models is a challenging task as they require large amounts of data and significant computation power to converge.

Training deep neural networks involves minimizing a loss function that measures the difference between the predicted outputs and the ground truth labels. However, due to their complex nature, these models tend to overfit to the training data, resulting in poor generalization and unstable training.

To overcome this issue, various techniques have been proposed to stabilize the training of generative AI models. These techniques aim to prevent overfitting and improve the overall performance of the model.

Regularization

Regularization is a widely used technique for stabilizing training in deep learning models. It involves adding extra terms to the loss function during training, which penalize large weights and encourages simpler models. This helps prevent overfitting by limiting the model's capacity to fit noise in the data.

Some common forms of regularization used in generative AI models are L1 and L2 regularization, which penalize the weights based on their absolute and squared values, respectively. Another popular form of regularization is Dropout, where a random subset of neurons is dropped during training to prevent co-adaptation. Regularization techniques play a crucial role in preventing overfitting and improving the generalization of deep learning models.

Batch Normalization

Batch normalization is another effective technique for stabilizing training in deep learning models.

It involves normalizing the activations of each layer before passing them to the next layer. This helps address issues with internal covariate shift, where the distribution of inputs to each layer changes during training. Batch normalization helps the model learn more stable and robust representations, leading to improved performance and faster convergence.

Data Augmentation

Data augmentation is a technique used to increase the diversity of data available for training. It involves creating new synthetic data points by applying transformations such as rotations, flips, or translations to existing data. By increasing the diversity of data, data augmentation can help prevent overfitting and improve the generalization of deep learning models. It is commonly used in computer vision tasks but can also be applied to other types of data such as audio or text.

Early Stopping

Early stopping is a regularization technique that involves monitoring the model's performance on a validation set during training. When the model's performance on the validation set starts to decrease, training is stopped early. This prevents the model from overfitting on the training data and allows it to generalize to new data better. Early stopping can be a useful technique when training deep learning models with limited computational resources or when dealing with large datasets.

Ensemble Learning

Ensemble learning involves combining multiple individual models to create a more powerful and robust model. This can be achieved through techniques such as bagging, boosting, or stacking. By combining the predictions of multiple models, ensemble learning can improve overall performance and reduce overfitting in deep learning models. Ensemble learning is often used in competitions and has been shown to produce state-of-the-art results in various tasks.

Transfer Learning

Transfer learning involves using pre-trained deep learning models on a specific task and fine-tuning them on a different but related task. This allows the model to transfer its knowledge from one domain to another, reducing the need for large amounts of data and training time. Transfer learning has been particularly successful in computer vision tasks, where pre-trained models trained on large datasets such as ImageNet have been used to achieve impressive results on new tasks with limited data. It is also becoming increasingly popular in other domains such as natural language processing and speech recognition. By utilizing transfer learning, deep learning models can be trained faster and achieve better performance on new tasks.

Challenges And Limitations

Mode Collapse

Machine learning has created a huge impact in the field of Artificial Intelligence. With its ability to learn and adapt, it has opened up new possibilities for creating intelligent systems. One such branch of machine learning is Generative AI, which focuses on generating content or data that resembles human-made content.

However, like any other technology, generative AI also comes with its own set of challenges and limitations. One of the major issues faced by generative AI is mode collapse.

Mode collapse refers to a scenario where the model learns only one specific output, ignoring all other variations of the input data. In simpler terms, it means that the AI system generates similar outputs for different inputs, resulting in a limited range of diversity in its generated content.

This limitation can greatly affect the quality and diversity of content generated by generative AI systems. It can also result in biased or incomplete outputs, as the model fails to capture the full range of possibilities.

To overcome mode collapse, researchers are exploring various techniques such as incorporating diversity-promoting loss functions and regularization methods. However, this is an ongoing challenge that requires further research and development.

Data Bias

Another major challenge faced by generative AI is data bias. Data bias refers to the distortion of training data, which results in biased outputs from the AI model. This can happen due to various factors such as a lack of diversity in the training data, inherent biases in the data collection process, or unintentional biases encoded in the algorithms used.

Data bias can have serious consequences, especially in applications where generative AI is used to generate content for decision-making processes. Biased outputs can lead to unfair or discriminatory decisions, and can perpetuate existing societal biases.

To address data bias in generative AI, researchers are working on developing methods to detect and mitigate biases in training data. This includes techniques such as incorporating diversity in the training data and actively monitoring and adjusting for biases during the training process.

Ethical Concerns

As generative AI systems continue to improve in their ability to generate content, ethical concerns have also emerged. One of the main concerns is the potential misuse of these systems, such as the creation of fake news or malicious content.

It is important for developers and researchers to consider the potential ethical implications of their work and implement safeguards to prevent malicious use of generative AI. This could include measures such as transparent disclosure of the use of AI in generated content, and implementing ethical guidelines for the training data used.

Another aspect that needs to be addressed is the potential impact of generative AI on employment. As these systems become more advanced, there is a concern that they may replace human workers in certain industries. It is important for society to have discussions and develop policies to address these potential impacts and ensure a fair transition.

Training Instability

One of the main challenges faced by generative AI is the issue of training instability. This refers to the difficulty in consistently producing high-quality results, as the AI model may sometimes fail to generate accurate or coherent outputs.

Training instability can occur due to various factors such as limited data availability, incorrect training methods, and overfitting. As a result, it can be challenging to create reliable and consistent generative AI models that can produce satisfactory results in different scenarios.

CHAPTER 4: GENERATIVE AI FOR BUSINESS

As businesses strive to stay competitive in the ever-evolving market, they are constantly exploring new technologies and innovative solutions to gain an edge over their competitors. One such technology that has gained significant traction in recent years is Generative Artificial Intelligence (Generative AI).

Generative AI refers to a subset of artificial intelligence that focuses on creating or generating content, rather than analyzing or understanding it. In simpler terms, Generative AI is used to produce new and unique content based on existing data.

Importance And Relevance For Businesses

The growing popularity of Generative AI in recent years can be attributed to its ability to automate and optimize various business processes, leading to increased efficiency and productivity. This technology enables businesses to generate new ideas and concepts faster than ever before, saving time and resources while also promoting innovation.

Moreover, Generative AI can also assist businesses in making accurate and data-driven decisions. By analyzing large volumes of data, this technology can identify patterns, trends, and insights that humans may not be able to detect. This information can then be used to make informed decisions about business strategies, product development, marketing campaigns, and more. This can ultimately lead to increased profitability and growth for businesses.

Another significant advantage of Generative AI is its potential to enhance customer experiences. By using data and algorithms, this technology can generate personalized content and recommendations for customers, improving their overall experience with a business. Moreover, it can also help in automating customer service processes such as chatbots, leading to quicker response times and improved customer satisfaction.

In addition to these practical applications, Generative AI also has the potential to drive innovation and creativity in various industries. By leveraging its ability to generate new ideas and concepts, businesses can develop innovative products and services that meet their customers' evolving needs. This can give them a competitive edge in the market, leading to long-term success.

Generative Models Overview

Generative models are a subset of machine learning algorithms that aim to create new data based on patterns and features found in existing data. These models use complex mathematical techniques such as deep learning and neural networks to generate new content, images, videos, or other types of data. They work by analyzing large datasets and learning their underlying structure to produce original outputs.

There are several types of generative models, including Variational Autoencoders (VAE), Generative Adversarial Networks (GANs), and Autoregressive models. Each type has its own unique approach to generating new data, but all rely on the same concept of learning from existing data.

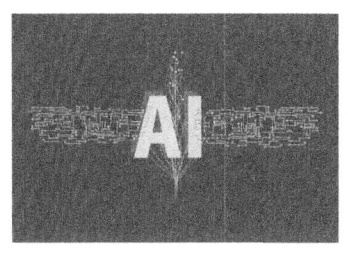

Types Of Generative Models Relevant To Business Applications

Generative models have gained significant attention in the business world due to their ability to generate new data similar to the training data they were trained on. This has opened up a range of possibilities for businesses, from generating synthetic data for research and testing purposes to creating personalized customer experiences.

Several types of generative models are relevant to business applications:

1. **Autoencoders:** These are neural networks trained to compress and then reconstruct

input data. They can be used for image or text generation, as they learn the underlying distribution of the data and can generate new samples accordingly.

2. **Generative Adversarial Networks (GANs):** GANs consist of two neural networks - a generator and a discriminator - that compete against each other. The generator creates new samples while the discriminator tries to distinguish between real and fake data. This results in highly realistic generated samples, making GANs useful for tasks such as image generation.

3. **Variational Autoencoders (VAEs):** Similar to autoencoders, VAEs are trained to encode input data into a latent space and then decode it back into the original data. However, VAEs also learn a probabilistic distribution of the latent space, allowing for the generation of new samples that may not be present in the training data.

4. **Recurrent Neural Networks (RNNs):** These are a type of deep learning model commonly used for sequential data such as text or time series data. RNNs can generate new text or time series data based on the patterns and relationships learned from the training data.

5. **Markov Chain Models:** These models

use probabilistic transitions between states to generate new sequences of data. They have been applied in various business applications such as natural language generation and recommendation systems.

Generative models have shown great potential in a variety of business and research applications. Many companies are using generative models to generate new product designs, create personalized content for customers, and even develop new drug molecules.

Applications In Marketing And Advertising

One growing application of AI in business is through generative models, particularly within the marketing and advertising industry. Generative models use deep learning algorithms to create new content based on existing data. This technology has revolutionized the way businesses approach content generation, from creating personalized ads to generating product descriptions.

Image And Video Generation For Campaigns

Image and Video generation is a key aspect of marketing and branding for businesses. The ability to create unique, high-quality visual content that resonates with the target audience can make all the difference in a successful campaign. With advancements in technology, businesses now have access to generative AI tools that use deep learning algorithms to automatically generate images and videos.

Generative AI is a subset of artificial intelligence that focuses on creating content such as images, videos, and text. These AI tools are trained on large datasets of existing visual content to learn the patterns and styles needed to generate new, unique variations. This means businesses can now produce endless amounts of brand-specific visuals without the need for a professional designer or videographer.

One major advantage of using generative AI for image and video generation is the speed at which content can be created. Traditional methods of creating visual content, such as hiring a designer or using stock images, can take days or even weeks to produce one piece of content. Generative AI tools, on the other hand, can generate hundreds of variations in just a matter of minutes.

Personalized Content Generation

With generative AI, businesses can take advantage of vast amounts of data to create targeted and personalized content that resonates with their audience. This is especially useful in today's digital age where customers are bombarded with generic marketing messages every day. With personalized content, businesses can cut through the noise and connect with their customers on a deeper level.

One of the most common uses of generative AI in business is in chatbots. These AI-powered assistants can generate responses to customer inquiries, providing personalized and timely answers without human intervention. This not only improves customer service but also frees up valuable time for businesses to focus on other tasks.

Another application of generative AI is in recommendation engines. By analyzing customer data, these systems can generate personalized product or content recommendations, increasing the chances of a sale or engagement. This has been proven to be highly effective, with companies like Netflix and Amazon using generative AI to improve their recommendation algorithms.

But perhaps one of the most exciting areas where generative AI is making an impact is in content creation. With the ability to analyze vast amounts of data and understand patterns, generative AI can assist in generating original content for businesses. This could include product reviews, social media posts, email campaigns, and even news articles.

Automated Creative Design

Generative artificial intelligence (GAI) is a subset of AI that focuses on creating, generating, or producing new content. It goes beyond traditional machine learning (ML) algorithms that are designed to recognize patterns in existing data and instead use algorithms to create original content. In recent years, generative AI has seen significant advancements in technology and has been applied in various industries such as art, music, fashion, and gaming.

In the business world, GAI has become a key tool for automated creative design, streamlining and enhancing the design process. By leveraging GAI algorithms, businesses are able to automate tasks that would otherwise require human input, saving time and resources while improving overall efficiency.

One of the most significant applications of GAI in business is in graphic design. Designers often have to create multiple versions of a single design, making minor changes or tweaks until the final design is approved. With GAI tools, designers can input basic parameters and let the algorithms generate a multitude of variations in seconds. This not only saves time but also allows for more creativity as designers can explore different options and combinations without being limited by traditional manual processes.

Another area where generative AI is transforming business is content marketing. GAI algorithms can analyze data from various sources such as social media, customer feedback, and online trends to create optimized and personalized content for different target audiences. This is especially useful for businesses with a large volume of content needs, such as e-commerce sites or news outlets.

In addition to aiding in the creative process, generative AI is also being used in business for predictive purposes. With access to vast amounts of data and advanced machine learning algorithms, GAI can analyze patterns and make predictions on future trends and behaviors. This helps businesses make more informed decisions and adapt to changes in the market.

Furthermore, generative AI is also being used in customer service through chatbots and virtual assistants. These intelligent systems use natural language processing and machine learning to understand and respond to customer inquiries in real-time, providing efficient and personalized support. This not only improves the overall customer experience but also frees up human employees to focus on more complex tasks.

Personalized Advertising

AI-powered generative models have opened up a whole new world of personalized advertising. By analyzing consumer data, these models can create tailored ads for each individual customer. This means that businesses can deliver ads that are more relevant and engaging to their target audience, leading to higher conversion rates and a better return on investment.

For example, a clothing brand can use generative

AI to create unique advertisements for different segments of their target market based on their preferences, browsing history, and purchase behavior. This could lead to more effective advertising campaigns and ultimately, increased sales.

Improved Content Creation

In addition to personalized ads, generative AI can also be used for content creation in marketing and advertising. Traditional methods of creating content can be time-consuming and costly. However, with generative models, businesses can quickly generate a large amount of content based on existing data. This can be particularly useful for tasks such as creating product descriptions or social media posts.

For instance, a travel company can use generative AI to automatically create unique descriptions for their destinations and activities. This not only saves time and resources, but also ensures that the content is tailored to each specific destination and its target audience.

Better Understanding of Consumer Behavior

Generative AI can also provide businesses with valuable insights into consumer behavior. By analyzing data from various sources, these models can identify patterns and trends in customer preferences, interests, and purchase behavior.

For example, a food delivery service can use generative AI to analyze customer data and identify which dishes are most popular among specific demographics. This information can then be used to create targeted promotions or even develop new menu items that cater to different consumer preferences.

Enhancing Customer Experience

Generative AI can be a game-changing technology for businesses seeking to enhance their customer experience. It is a type of artificial intelligence that uses machine learning algorithms to generate new and unique content, such as text, images, or videos.

With the rise of digital technologies and social media, customers have come to expect personalized and engaging experiences from businesses. Generative AI can help companies meet these expectations by creating tailored and compelling content for different customer segments.

For example, a clothing brand could use generative AI to create personalized fashion recommendations for each of its customers based on their style preferences, previous purchases, and browsing history. This not only improves the overall shopping experience for the customer but also increases the likelihood of making a sale for the business.

Another way generative AI can enhance customer experience is through chatbots. These virtual assistants use natural language processing and generative AI to interact with customers and provide real-time assistance. They can answer frequently asked questions, make product recommendations, and even handle basic transactions. This streamlines the customer service process, making it more efficient and convenient for both the customer and the business.

Generative AI can also be used to create more interactive and engaging social media content. For example, a company could use generative algorithms to generate personalized videos or images for each customer, showcasing how their product would look in their own unique environment. This not only grabs the attention of potential customers but also makes them feel valued and connected with the brand.

In addition to enhancing customer experience, generative AI can also improve internal business processes. By automating tedious and repetitive tasks, employees can focus on more high-value work, leading to increased productivity and efficiency. For instance, generative AI can analyze data and generate reports or create personalized marketing campaigns based on customer behavior patterns.

Chatbots

Chatbots are computer programs designed to simulate conversation with human users through text, voice commands, or both. They use natural language processing and machine learning algorithms to understand and respond to user queries in a conversational manner. Chatbots can be built for various purposes, such as customer service, sales assistance, or providing information. With the advancements in artificial intelligence (AI), chatbots have become increasingly intelligent, making them an essential tool for businesses in today's digital age.

Why Are Chatbots Beneficial For Businesses?

Chatbots have several benefits for businesses, including:

1. 24/7 Availability: Unlike human employees who have fixed working hours, chatbots can assist customers and provide information round-the-clock. This helps in improving customer satisfaction and reducing wait times.
2. Cost-Efficiency: Chatbots can handle multiple conversations simultaneously, reducing the need for businesses to hire or assign more employees to customer service roles. This helps in saving costs for businesses.
3. Personalization: With AI capabilities,

chatbots can personalize user interactions by understanding their preferences and providing tailored responses. This improves the overall customer experience and builds brand loyalty.

4. Increased Efficiency: Chatbots can quickly analyze and respond to user queries, reducing the response time and increasing efficiency. This helps in freeing up human employees from repetitive tasks, allowing them to focus on more complex and critical tasks.

5. Scalability: As businesses grow, they can easily scale chatbot services without worrying about hiring more employees or training them. This makes chatbots a cost-effective and scalable solution for businesses.

6. Data Collection: Chatbots can collect valuable user data, such as preferences, buying patterns, and feedback. This data can be analyzed and used to improve business strategies and personalize future interactions with customers.

7. Multilingual Support: With advancements in natural language processing (NLP), chatbots can communicate in multiple languages, making it easier for businesses to expand globally and cater to a diverse customer

base.
8. Integration with Other Platforms: Chatbots can be integrated with various messaging platforms, social media channels, and websites, providing a seamless customer service experience across multiple channels.
9. Continuous Improvement: With machine learning capabilities, chatbots can continuously learn from user interactions and improve their responses over time. This ensures that the chatbot is always up-to-date and can provide accurate and relevant information to users.

Natural Language Generation For Customer Interaction

Chatbots are not just limited to answering customer queries, but they can also generate personalized responses in natural language. This means that chatbots can communicate with customers using human-like language and provide a more engaging and personalized experience.

Natural Language Generation (NLG) is a subset of artificial intelligence (AI) that enables computers to convert data into text automatically. It uses advanced algorithms to understand and analyze data and then generates human-like text based on the insights derived from the data.

NLG allows chatbots to respond in a conversational manner, making interactions with customers more natural and efficient. This not only improves customer satisfaction but also saves time and resources for businesses. Moreover, NLG can generate responses in multiple languages, further enhancing the global reach of chatbots.

In addition to customer interactions, NLG can also be used for creating personalized content such as product descriptions, marketing emails, and social media posts. This further streamlines business processes and reduces the need for human intervention.

Customized Product Recommendations

Chatbots with machine learning capabilities can also provide personalized product recommendations to customers based on their preferences and past interactions. This not only helps in improving customer satisfaction but also increases sales for businesses.

With access to a vast amount of data, chatbots can analyze customer behavior and patterns to understand their interests and needs. They can then suggest products that are more likely to be purchased by the customer, increasing the chances of conversion.

Moreover, chatbots can also learn from each interaction and continuously improve their recommendations to provide even more personalized suggestions to customers.

CHAPTER 5: UNDERSTANDING DATA AUGMENTATION

Data augmentation is a technique used to artificially increase the amount of training data by creating new data from existing data. It is commonly used in machine learning and deep learning to improve the performance of models and reduce overfitting.

The Importance Of Data Augmentation For Businesses

For businesses, data augmentation offers several benefits. Firstly, it allows them to train their AI systems on a more diverse range of data, which can lead to better generalization and improved accuracy. This is particularly useful for businesses that operate in diverse markets or have a wide range of customers.

Secondly, data augmentation can help businesses save time and money. By generating new data from existing data, businesses can reduce the costs associated with collecting and labeling large amounts of new data. This makes it easier and more affordable to train AI systems on different datasets.

Techniques For Data Augmentation

There are several techniques that can be used for

data augmentation, depending on the type of data and the specific needs of a business. Some popular techniques include:

1. Image Augmentation: This involves modifying images by applying transformations such as rotation, flipping, scaling, and cropping. It is commonly used in computer vision applications.
2. Text Augmentation: This technique involves generating new sentences or phrases by replacing words with synonyms, adding noise, or shuffling the order of words. It is useful for natural language processing tasks.
3. Audio Augmentation: Similar to image augmentation, audio augmentation involves altering audio data by changing pitch, speed, or volume to create new samples. This technique is commonly used in speech recognition and audio classification tasks.

Best Practices For Data Augmentation

To get the most out of data augmentation, businesses should follow some best practices. These include:

1. Understanding the Data: Before applying any data augmentation techniques, it is important to thoroughly understand the

dataset and its characteristics. This will help determine which techniques are suitable and how much augmentation is needed.
2. Balancing Quality and Quantity: While data augmentation can generate a large amount of new data, it is important to strike a balance between quantity and quality. Generating too many variations can lead to overfitting and decrease the performance of AI models.
3. Evaluating the Performance: It is crucial to evaluate the performance of AI models after applying data augmentation techniques. This will help determine whether the augmented data has helped improve the accuracy or other metrics.
4. Combining Techniques: Data augmentation techniques can be combined to generate more diverse data samples. For example, image rotation and flipping can be used together to create new images with different angles and orientations.
5. Keeping the Original Dataset: It is always recommended to keep the original dataset separate from the augmented data. This will help compare the performance of AI models trained on both datasets and determine the effectiveness of data augmentation.

6. Updating Regularly: As AI models continue to learn from new data, it is important to regularly update the augmented dataset with fresh data. This will help prevent overfitting and maintain the accuracy of AI models.

In addition to these best practices, some specific techniques can be used for different types of data:

1. Image Data Augmentation: Techniques such as rotation, flipping, cropping, and color manipulation can be used to create variations of images. This is especially useful for image classification tasks where the AI model needs to recognize objects from different angles and backgrounds.
2. Text Data Augmentation: For text data, techniques such as synonym replacement, word embedding, and back translation can be used to generate new texts with slightly different meanings or contexts. This can improve the performance of AI models for tasks such as sentiment analysis and text classification.
3. Audio Data Augmentation: Techniques such as time shifting, pitch shifting, and background noise addition can be used to create variations of audio data. This is beneficial for speech recognition tasks

where the AI model needs to recognize speech in various environments and accents.
4. Tabular Data Augmentation: For tabular data, techniques such as feature scaling, imputation, and sampling can be used to create new variations of the existing dataset. This can improve the performance of AI models for tasks such as regression and classification.

Limitations And Challenges

Data augmentation is a powerful tool for improving the performance of generative AI models. However, like any other technique, it has its limitations and challenges that need to be considered when incorporating it into a business strategy.

1. Availability Of Data

The success of data augmentation heavily relies on the availability of diverse and representative data. In some industries or applications, obtaining such data may be a challenge. For example, in medical imaging, obtaining large and diverse datasets can be difficult due to privacy concerns and the complexity of acquiring medical images.

2. Domain-specific Considerations

Data augmentation techniques need to be tailored for specific domains and applications. What works for image data may not necessarily work for text data or audio data. Therefore, businesses must carefully consider which techniques are appropriate for their specific domain and data type.

3. Computational Resources

Applying certain data augmentation methods can be computationally intensive, especially when working with large datasets. This may require businesses to invest in more powerful hardware or cloud computing services, which can add to the overall cost of implementing generative AI.

4. Robustness Of Generated Data

Data augmentation can generate new data points that are slightly different from the original ones. While this can be beneficial for training models, it could also lead to overfitting and unreliable results if not done carefully. Therefore, businesses must carefully evaluate the robustness of the generated data before incorporating it into their models.

5. Balancing Quality And Quantity

One of the challenges of data augmentation is finding the right balance between increasing the quantity of data and maintaining its quality. Simply generating a large amount of low-quality data may not lead to improved model performance. Therefore, businesses must carefully consider the trade-offs between quantity and quality when using data augmentation techniques.

6. Monitoring And Maintenance

Data augmentation is not a one-time process but rather an ongoing effort. As new data is collected, businesses must monitor and maintain their augmented datasets to ensure they are still relevant and effective in improving model performance. This requires a dedicated team or resources to continually evaluate and adjust the augmentation techniques used.

Synthetic Data Generation

Benefits Of Synthetic Data Generation

Improved Data Diversity For Training Models

One of the major roadblocks AI and machine learning (ML) initiatives face is ensuring a robust and diverse dataset for training models. Synthetic data generation offers a revolutionary approach, providing a wide variety of instances that might not occur naturally in collected datasets. By utilizing generative models, enterprises can now expose their systems to a broader spectrum of real-world possibilities, capable of enhancing model performance under diverse scenarios.

Cost-Effective Data Augmentation

The cost of collecting and labeling data can be exorbitant. Synthetic data, on the other hand, can be produced and manipulated at a fraction of the price. This financial advantage allows businesses, particularly startups and small enterprises, to significantly reduce the barriers to entry for AI adoption. Data synthesis not only saves resources traditionally spent on data acquisition but also provides a competitive edge by accelerating the pace of model development and deployment.

Enhanced Data Privacy And Security

In the era of stringent data protection regulations and increasing privacy concerns, synthetic data stands out as a privacy-friendly alternative. With generative AI, organizations can create datasets that are entirely fictional yet statistically similar to their real data, thereby decreasing the risk of privacy breaches and the regulatory burdens that come with real data handling.

Applications In Business

Use Cases Across Different Sectors

The deployment of synthetic data generation is transcending industry boundaries, finding applications in sectors as diverse as healthcare, finance, marketing, and beyond.

1. In healthcare, synthetic data is invaluable for training medical image analysis models without compromising

patient data. It can also simulate patient profiles and disease pathways for drug development and treatment optimization.
2. The financial sector leverages synthetic data for regulatory testing, fraud detection, and creating stress testing models.
3. Marketing benefits from the customizability of synthetic data, enabling detailed segmentation analysis and marketing campaign simulation.

Impact on Decision-Making and Operations Efficiency

Business processes are increasingly driven by data. The high-quality, customized nature of synthetic data allows for better-informed decisions, improving strategy and operations efficiency. Models trained on synthetic data can account for an extensive range of factors, leading to more accurate predictions and optimization of resources.

Challenges And Considerations

Data Quality and Reliability Issues

Despite its benefits, synthetic data is only as good as the models that generate it. Issues related to data quality and reliability, stemming from the inadequacies of these models, are paramount. Enterprises need to devise stringent validation processes to ensure that the synthetic data reflects real-world conditions accurately.

Integration Hurdles And Technical Requirements

Integrating synthetic data into existing systems without disrupting operations is a technical challenge that requires careful planning and significant technical investment. IT and data science teams need to work in tandem to develop robust solutions that seamlessly bridge the gap between synthetic and real data.

Design Prototyping And Iteration

Design prototyping and iteration are crucial elements in developing generative AI for business. These methods help businesses to create effective prototypes, test different design ideas, and identify potential issues before investing in the full development process.

The first step in design prototyping is creating a prototype that simulates the end product or mimics its functionality. This can be done using software tools or even physical mockups. The aim is to create a representation of the final product that can be tested and evaluated by stakeholders or potential users.

Once the prototype is created, businesses can conduct user testing to gather feedback and identify any areas for improvement. This is an essential step as it allows businesses to understand how users interact with their products and make necessary changes before moving on to full development.

Design iteration, on the other hand, involves making small incremental changes to a prototype or product based on user feedback and testing. This process allows businesses to refine their design and address any issues that may have been identified during the prototyping phase.

Open Data Sets

When it comes to training a Generative AI model, having access to large and diverse data sets is crucial. Open data sets are publicly available databases that provide high-quality data for machine learning purposes. These datasets can range from small datasets with a few hundred samples to massive datasets with millions of samples.

Open data sets can be found in various domains, such as text, images, audio, and more. Some popular open data sets for image generation include ImageNet, COCO (Common Objects in Context), and CIFAR-10 (Canadian Institute for Advanced Research). These datasets contain millions of labeled images that can be used to train Generative AI models.

However, it's important to note that not all open data sets are suitable for every type of Generative

AI model. For example, an open data set of images of animals may not be the best choice for training a text generation model.

Data Sharing and Collaboration

One of the biggest advantages of open data sets is that they promote data sharing and collaboration in the AI community. By making high-quality data sets publicly available, researchers and developers can access a diverse range of data to train their models.

Collaboration among different individuals or teams working on similar projects can also lead to new insights and advancements in the field of Generative AI. By sharing their findings and techniques, researchers can help improve the overall quality of models trained on open data sets.

Data Management

Despite the benefits, there are also challenges when it comes to using open data sets for Generative AI. One of the main challenges is managing and organizing the data in a way that is suitable for training.

Large open data sets can be difficult to navigate and may require significant preprocessing before they are ready to be used in model training. This requires expertise and resources, which may not be accessible to everyone.

To address these challenges, there are now

platforms and tools that help with data management for Generative AI. These include data labeling and annotation software, as well as data cleaning and preprocessing tools.

CHAPTER 6: LEGAL DOCUMENT GENERATION

Legal Document Generation

With the advancements in Artificial Intelligence (AI) technology, many industries have already started to integrate AI into their daily operations. One of the most notable applications is legal document generation. This process involves using AI algorithms to automatically generate legal documents such as contracts, agreements, and other forms.

This new approach has shown great potential in streamlining and improving the efficiency of legal processes. Here are some of the benefits and applications of using generative AI for legal document generation:

Applications Of Generative AI In Legal Document Generation

1. **Automated Contract Creation:** With the use of generative AI, companies and law firms can now easily generate contracts without having to manually draft them. The AI algorithms can analyze data from previous contracts, legal databases, and other sources to create accurate and customized contracts based on specific

requirements.
2. **Efficient Agreement Review:** In the past, reviewing agreements and contracts was a time-consuming process that required lawyers to go through hundreds of pages manually. Now, with generative AI, this task can be done in seconds. The algorithms can quickly analyze and compare different versions of agreements, highlight changes and discrepancies, and provide accurate summaries for review.
3. **Risk Analysis:** With the use of AI, legal teams can now analyze the potential risks and implications of a contract before it is signed. This helps them identify any loopholes or areas that may need further clarification, reducing the chances of disputes or legal complications in the future.
4. **Legal Research:** Another application of generative AI in legal document generation is assisting with legal research. With vast amounts of data available online, it can be a daunting task for lawyers to find relevant information. AI algorithms can quickly sift through large volumes of data, sort and categorize it, and provide accurate results for research purposes.

Benefits Of Generative AI In Legal Document Generation

1. **Time-saving:** One of the main benefits of using generative AI in legal document generation is the time saved. With automated document creation, lawyers no longer have to spend hours drafting contracts or agreements. This frees up their time to focus on other important tasks and increases productivity.
2. **Cost-effective:** By automating the document generation process, firms can save a significant amount of money that would otherwise be spent on hiring additional staff or outsourcing legal work. AI-powered document generation is a cost-effective solution for law firms of all sizes.
3. **Accuracy and Consistency:** AI algorithms are designed to be highly accurate and consistent in their output. This ensures that the generated documents are error-free and adhere to all legal requirements, reducing the chances of disputes or errors in the future.
4. **Improved Efficiency:** With AI handling document generation, lawyers can focus on higher-level tasks such as negotiating and strategizing, improving overall efficiency. This allows them to take

on more cases and clients, leading to increased revenue for the firm.

5. **Easy Collaboration:** Generative AI tools allow for easy collaboration among team members as multiple users can access and work on the same document simultaneously. This streamlines the document creation process, especially in situations where multiple lawyers or departments are involved.

6. **Customizable Templates:** AI-powered document generation tools allow for the creation of customizable templates that can be tailored to specific needs and requirements. This not only saves time but also ensures that all documents generated are consistent in format and style.

7. **Secure Storage:** With traditional document creation, there is always a risk of files being lost or damaged. Generative AI tools store documents securely in the cloud, reducing the risk of data loss or breach.

8. **24/7 Availability:** AI-powered document generation tools are available 24/7, allowing lawyers to generate documents anytime, anywhere. This is particularly useful in urgent situations where time is of the essence.

Automated Creation Of Legal Documents

In today's fast-paced business world, the creation of legal documents is a time-consuming and costly process. Legal teams are often overwhelmed with the amount of paperwork they have to generate for different clients and cases. This not only slows down the overall efficiency of operations but also leaves room for human error.

To address this challenge, businesses are turning to generative AI technology for the automated creation of legal documents. This technology allows for the quick and accurate generation of contracts, agreements, and other legal documents with minimal human involvement.

Compliance Reporting Automation

Businesses of all types and sizes are required to comply with federal, state, and local laws and regulations. This includes providing accurate and timely compliance reports to regulatory agencies. However, the process of generating these reports can be time-consuming and resource-intensive.

Enter generative AI for business. With this technology, businesses can automate the process of compliance reporting by using algorithms to analyze data, identify relevant regulations, and generate accurate reports. This not only saves time and resources but also reduces the risk of errors or non-compliance.

Contract Generation

In addition to compliance reporting, businesses also have a need to generate legal documents such as contracts. These documents are essential for outlining terms and agreements between parties involved in a business transaction.

Generative AI can streamline this process by analyzing relevant data and using natural language generation algorithms to create personalized contracts that meet the specific needs of each party. This eliminates the need for manual drafting and reviewing, saving time and reducing the risk of errors.

Intellectual Property Filings

Protecting intellectual property is crucial for businesses, but the filing process for patents, trademarks, and copyrights can be complex and tedious. Generative AI can assist in this area by automating the drafting of legal documents related to intellectual property filings.

By analyzing existing patents and trademarks, generative AI algorithms can generate accurate and comprehensive applications for businesses, saving time and resources while ensuring compliance with legal requirements.

Employee Agreements

Employee agreements are another important aspect of running a business. These documents outline the terms and conditions of employment and are essential for protecting both the employer and the employee.

Generative AI can assist in this area by analyzing relevant laws and regulations, as well as the company's policies, to generate personalized employment agreements that adhere to legal requirements. This not only saves time but also ensures compliance with labor laws.

Generating Reports For Regulatory Agencies And Internal Audits

Compliance with regulations and internal policies is crucial for businesses to avoid legal and financial consequences. Generative AI can assist in this area by automating the generation of reports for regulatory agencies and internal audits.

By analyzing relevant data and regulations, generative AI algorithms can generate accurate and comprehensive reports that meet compliance requirements. This reduces the risk of errors and saves time compared to manual report generation.

Conducting Legal Research

Legal research is a time-consuming and complex process that is essential for ensuring compliance with laws and regulations. Generative AI can assist in this area by analyzing relevant case law, legislation, and other legal resources to provide quick and accurate research results.

This not only saves time but also ensures that businesses have access to the most up-to-date and relevant legal information. Additionally, generative AI can assist in summarizing and organizing large amounts of legal data for easy analysis and decision-making.

How Generative AI Works

Generative AI technology uses algorithms to analyze data from existing legal documents and learn patterns and structures commonly used in such documents. This data is then combined with natural language processing (NLP) capabilities to generate new documents that are customized to meet the specific needs of a company or legal team. These documents are created in a matter of seconds, reducing the time and resources required for document creation.

Steps Involved In The Automated Creation Process

The following are the general steps involved in the automated creation of legal documents using generative AI technology:

Input Data

The input data for the generative AI tool can come from various sources. This can include existing legal documents, templates, company policies and procedures, industry regulations, and other structured data. The more diverse and relevant the input data is, the more accurate and comprehensive the generated document will be.

Analysis and Learning

During this stage, the generative AI tool uses advanced algorithms to analyze the input data. This involves identifying patterns, structures, and language used in the data. The tool also learns from the input data, using this information to generate a document that is tailored to fit specific requirements.

Customization

One of the key benefits of generative AI technology is its ability to customize documents according to various needs. This can include adjusting language to fit a certain tone or style, changing the structure of the document to adhere to specific guidelines, and incorporating specific information or data into the document.

Review And Approval

While generative AI technology is highly advanced, it is still important for a legal team or individual to review and approve the generated document. This ensures accuracy and completeness, as well as compliance with relevant laws and regulations.

Final Output

After any necessary revisions, the final version of the document is produced in a matter of seconds, ready for use. This not only saves time and resources but also ensures consistent and high-quality documents every time. Additionally, the generative AI tool can be continuously trained and improved upon to provide even more precise and effective results. As technology continues to advance, generative AI is becoming an increasingly valuable tool for the legal industry. It streamlines and speeds up document generation while maintaining accuracy and compliance, allowing legal professionals to focus on higher-value tasks. In the future, we can expect to see even more advancements in this technology, further revolutionizing the legal documentation process.

Risk Assessment And Management

In today's world, businesses are facing an increasing amount of legal documentation requirements. From contracts and agreements to compliance documents and regulatory filings, the demand for accurate, thorough and timely legal documentation is higher than ever before.

However, the traditional method of manual document generation can be time-consuming, error-prone and expensive. This is where Generative Artificial Intelligence (Generative AI) comes into play.

Generative AI refers to the use of artificial

intelligence and machine learning algorithms to create new content or documents based on a set of parameters or input data. In the context of legal document generation, Generative AI can transform the way businesses approach risk assessment and management.

Risk Assessment

Risk assessment is a crucial aspect of any business, especially in today's fast-paced and ever-changing market. It involves identifying potential risks that may impact the business operations, finances or reputation and implementing measures to mitigate them.

Traditionally, risk assessment was done manually by reviewing past incidents, analyzing data and making informed decisions based on expert knowledge. However, Generative AI can enhance this process by analyzing large amounts of data in a fraction of the time it would take for a human to do so. This can help businesses identify potential risks more accurately and efficiently, leading to better risk management strategies.

Risk Management

Once potential risks have been identified through the use of Generative AI, businesses can then focus on implementing effective risk management strategies. This may include creating and updating policies and procedures, monitoring compliance, and utilizing predictive analytics to anticipate potential risks.

Moreover, Generative AI can also assist in creating and updating legal documents such as contracts, agreements and policies. By analyzing past data and understanding the business's specific needs and goals, Generative AI can generate customized legal documents that are tailored to the business's unique risk profile. This not only saves time and reduces errors but also ensures that businesses have comprehensive and up-to-date risk management policies in place.

Changing The Risk Management Landscape

The integration of Generative AI in risk assessment and management has transformed the way businesses approach risk. With its ability to analyze large amounts of data, make accurate predictions and generate customized solutions, Generative AI has made risk management more efficient, effective and reliable.

It has also shifted the role of risk managers from solely relying on their expert knowledge and experience to becoming partners with AI technology. This partnership allows for a more holistic approach to risk management, combining both human intuition and advanced technological capabilities.

Generative AI has also enabled businesses to proactively manage risks rather than simply reacting when they occur. By predicting potential risks in advance, businesses can take preventative measures and mitigate the impact of these risks before they even happen.

Using Generative Models For Risk Prediction And Analysis

Generative AI models have the potential to revolutionize risk prediction and analysis. By analyzing vast amounts of data, these models can identify patterns and trends that humans may miss, allowing for more accurate risk predictions.

In addition, Generative AI's ability to simulate possible scenarios can aid in decision-making by providing insights into the potential impact of different risk management strategies.

The use of Generative AI in risk prediction and analysis also allows for a more proactive approach to risk management. Rather than simply reacting when risks occur, businesses can use these models to anticipate potential risks and take preventative measures.

Identifying Potential Legal And Compliance Risks In Business Operations

Legal and compliance risks are a major concern for businesses of all sizes. Generative AI can help identify potential legal and compliance risks in business operations by analyzing data from various sources, including contracts, regulatory filings, and case law.

By identifying patterns and anomalies in the data, Generative AI can alert businesses to potential issues before they become full-blown risks. This can save businesses time and money by avoiding legal disputes and regulatory fines.

In addition, Generative AI can assist businesses in remaining compliant with constantly changing regulations by continuously monitoring data and updating risk models accordingly.

Leveraging Generative Models For Cybersecurity Risk Management

Cybersecurity risks are a growing concern for businesses as the reliance on technology increases. Generative AI can help identify potential cybersecurity risks by analyzing large amounts of data, such as network logs, user behaviors, and system vulnerabilities.

By continuously learning from new data, Generative AI can detect anomalies and potential threats in real-time. This allows businesses to take swift action to prevent cyber attacks before they occur.

Furthermore, Generative AI can be used to simulate potential cyber-attack scenarios and test the effectiveness of different security measures. This helps businesses proactively strengthen their cybersecurity defenses and mitigate potential risks.

Future Possibilities

As technology continues to advance and Generative AI capabilities expand, the possibilities for its use in risk management are endless. Some potential future applications include:

1. Real-time risk assessment: With the ability to analyze data in real-time, Generative AI could be used to continuously monitor and identify potential risks as they arise, allowing for immediate action to be taken.
2. Automated risk reporting: Rather than manually compiling and analyzing data for risk reports, Generative AI could generate comprehensive and customized reports automatically.
3. Personalized risk management solutions: With its ability to process large amounts of data, Generative AI can create personalized risk management solutions tailored specifically to a business's unique risk profile.

CHAPTER 7: OVERCOMING CHALLENGES AND RISK

Overcoming Challenges And Risk

With the growing demand for advanced technology and automation in business operations, generative artificial intelligence (AI) has become a popular choice for many organizations. It involves using algorithms to generate new ideas, content, or designs that mimic human creativity. However, like any other emerging technology, there are challenges and risks associated with implementing generative AI in business.

Technical Challenges

One of the main challenges in using generative AI for business is the technical complexity involved. Developing and implementing these algorithms requires a high level of expertise and specialized skills, which can be costly for companies that do not have an in-house team with such capabilities. Additionally, maintaining and updating these technologies can also be challenging as it involves continuous monitoring, debugging, and optimization.

Dealing With Mode Collapse In Generative Adversarial Networks (GANs)

GANs are a popular type of generative AI that involves two neural networks competing against each other to generate new data. However, one common challenge with GANs is mode collapse, where the generator network only learns to produce variations of a limited number of patterns from the training data. This results in repetitive and unoriginal outputs, limiting the potential for novel and diverse ideas.

Addressing Training Instability And Convergence Issues

Another technical challenge with generative AI is the stability and convergence of algorithms during training. Due to the high-dimensional nature of data, these algorithms can easily get stuck in local minima or fail to converge at all. This can lead to low-quality outputs and hinder the potential for creativity and innovation.

Handling Large-Scale Data Requirements And Computational Resources

Generative AI algorithms often require large amounts of training data to produce high-quality outputs. This can be a challenge for businesses that do not have access to such vast amounts of data or the computational resources needed to process it. Moreover, as the size and complexity of data continue to increase, these challenges will only become more significant.

Ethical And Bias-Related Challenges

With the increasing use of AI in business, it is crucial to address the ethical and bias-related challenges that arise with generative AI.

Ethical Challenges:

One of the biggest ethical challenges of generative AI is its potential to perpetuate bias and discrimination. This can happen when the data used to train the AI models contains inherent biases, such as gender or racial biases. If these biases are not identified and addressed, the AI will continue to replicate them, leading to discriminatory outcomes.

Another ethical challenge is the lack of transparency in how generative AI makes decisions. Unlike traditional computer programs where the code can be easily reviewed, generative AI uses complex algorithms that are difficult for humans to understand. This lack of transparency can make it challenging to identify and address any biases that may be present in the AI.

Moreover, generative AI can also raise ethical concerns about data privacy. As these models are trained on large datasets containing sensitive information, there is a risk of this information being used for unintended purposes.

Ethical Considerations In Data Collection And Usage:

To overcome ethical challenges, businesses must carefully consider the data used to train generative AI models. It is vital to ensure that the datasets are representative and free from biases. This can be achieved by diversifying the teams involved in collecting and labeling the data.

Additionally, businesses must also establish clear guidelines for how the AI will be used and its limitations. This can help prevent unintended consequences and ensure that the AI is used ethically.

Furthermore, data privacy must be a top priority when working with generative AI. Businesses must establish strict protocols for how data is collected, stored, and used to protect individuals' privacy rights.

Bias-Related Challenges:

Generative AI can also face challenges related to bias in its outputs. This can occur when the AI is trained on historical data that may be biased. For example, if a company's hiring decisions in the past were based on gender or race, then a generative AI model trained on this data may also exhibit these biases and perpetuate them in its decision-making.

Another bias-related challenge is the lack of diversity in the teams developing and implementing generative AI models. If the teams are not diverse, they may not be able to identify and address biases in the AI effectively.

Potential Solutions:

To combat these ethical and bias-related challenges, it is crucial for organizations using generative AI to prioritize diversity and inclusion in their teams. This can help bring different perspectives that can identify and mitigate biases in AI.

Additionally, there should also be a focus on transparency in how generative AI makes decisions. This includes creating accessible documentation and explanations of the algorithms used, as well as actively monitoring and auditing the AI to identify any potential biases.

Furthermore, ethical guidelines and regulations should be put in place to ensure that generative AI is developed and implemented responsibly. These guidelines can also address issues such as data privacy and accountability.

Ensuring Transparency And Explainability In Generative AI Systems:

Transparency and explainability are crucial aspects of developing responsible generative AI systems. This means that the inner workings of the AI should be understandable and able to be explained to the user or stakeholder.

One potential solution for achieving transparency is through the use of interpretable models, which allow for an easier understanding of how the AI makes decisions. These models can also help identify any potential biases in the AI. Additionally, providing documentation and explanations on how data is collected and used can also increase transparency.

Explainability can be achieved through techniques such as post-hoc explanations, which provide insights into how the AI arrived at its decisions. These explanations can also help identify any biases present in the AI.

Data Quality And Diversity

One of the major challenges is ensuring data quality and diversity. Generative AI systems rely heavily on trained data sets to create outputs, whether it's text, images, or audio. If the data is biased, incomplete, or not diverse enough, it can lead to inaccurate and even harmful results. This can have serious consequences for businesses, especially in industries such as healthcare and finance.

To overcome this challenge, organizations must prioritize data quality and diversity when collecting and preparing training data for their generative AI systems. They should also regularly monitor and audit the data to identify any biases or gaps and make necessary adjustments to improve the overall quality and diversity of their data sets.

Ensuring Data Quality For Effective Model Training

Another challenge with generative AI is ensuring data quality for effective model training. The success of a generative AI system depends on the accuracy and relevance of the data it is trained on. If the data is noisy or contains errors, it can lead to poor performance and unreliable outputs.

Organizations should have robust processes in place to ensure the quality of their training data, such as data cleaning and validation techniques. They should also consider using diverse sources of data to improve the overall quality and diversity of their training sets.

Dealing With Limited Or Biased Training Data

Limited or biased training data is another challenge for businesses implementing generative AI. In some cases, the required data may not be readily available, or it may be biased towards certain demographics or groups. This can result in models that do not accurately represent the real-world and produce biased outputs.

To overcome this challenge, organizations must actively seek out diverse and relevant sources of training data, and consider using techniques such as data augmentation to increase the diversity of their data sets. They should also regularly review and audit their training data for biases, and make necessary adjustments to ensure fairness and accuracy in their models.

Strategies For Data Augmentation And Synthetic Data Generation

Data augmentation and synthetic data generation are techniques used to increase the diversity and quantity of training data. These techniques involve creating new data points by modifying or combining existing ones, or generating entirely new data using algorithms.

Some commonly used methods for data augmentation include rotation, flipping, and adding noise to images or text. Synthetic data generation involves using generative models to create realistic-looking but artificial data points. This can be especially useful when dealing with limited or sensitive training data.

Organizations must carefully select and implement these techniques based on their specific needs and the type of data they are working with. They must also ensure that the generated data is representative of the real world and does not introduce any biases into their models.

Importance Of Data Cleaning And Validation Techniques

In addition to data augmentation and synthetic data generation, organizations must also prioritize data cleaning and validation techniques as part of their data preparation process. This involves identifying and removing any incomplete, duplicate, or irrelevant data points from the training set.

Data cleaning and validation are essential for ensuring the quality and accuracy of the training data, which ultimately impacts the performance of the resulting model. It also helps to identify any potential biases in the data and address them before training the model.

Moreover, as organizations continue to collect more and more data, it becomes crucial to regularly clean and validate the data to maintain its integrity. This can help prevent errors or inaccuracies from creeping into the training set over time.

Regulatory Compliance

One major challenge when implementing AI in business is regulatory compliance. With increasing concerns about data privacy and security, there are strict regulations in place that businesses must adhere to when using AI. For example, the General Data Protection Regulation (GDPR) in Europe requires organizations to gain explicit consent from individuals before collecting their personal data for AI purposes.

In addition to GDPR, there may be industry-specific regulations that businesses need to comply with when using AI. This can make it difficult for businesses to effectively use AI without violating any regulations.

To overcome this challenge, businesses need to carefully evaluate and understand the regulatory landscape that applies to their industry. This includes staying up-to-date with any changes in regulations and ensuring that all data used for AI is collected and stored in a compliant manner. It may also involve seeking additional certifications or conducting audits to ensure compliance.

Navigating Legal And Regulatory Frameworks Applicable To Generative AI

In addition to regulatory compliance, businesses also need to navigate the legal and regulatory frameworks that apply specifically to generative AI. This involves understanding intellectual property laws, licensing agreements, and potential ethical concerns surrounding the use of AI.

For example, if a business is using generative AI to create original content such as music or art, there may be copyright laws and licensing agreements in place that need to be considered. This can also apply to the use of existing data sets, as businesses must ensure they have the legal rights to use and manipulate that data.

Compliance Requirements For Data Usage, Privacy And Fairness

As AI continues to evolve and become more widespread, there will likely be further regulations put in place to govern its usage. In addition to GDPR, organizations should also keep an eye on upcoming regulations such as the ePrivacy Regulation and the EU Data Protection Board's guidelines on data protection impact assessments.

These regulations focus on protecting individuals' personal information from being misused or exploited by AI systems. This includes ensuring transparency in data usage, providing individuals with the right to access and control their personal data, and mitigating any potential bias or discrimination in AI decision-making processes.

Ensuring Alignment With Industry Standards And Best Practices

In addition to legal and regulatory compliance, businesses also need to consider industry standards and best practices when implementing generative AI. This involves staying up-to-date with evolving technologies, understanding potential risks and vulnerabilities, and following ethical guidelines for responsible AI development.

Organizations can also seek guidance from professional organizations and associations that specialize in AI, such as the Partnership on AI or IEEE Global Initiative on Ethics of Autonomous and Intelligent Systems. Adhering to these standards and best practices not only ensures compliance, but also helps build trust with stakeholders and promotes responsible and ethical use of AI technology.

User Acceptance And Trust

One of the biggest challenges facing Generative AI is gaining user acceptance and trust. This is because people are often hesitant to rely on technology to generate original content, as it can be difficult to determine its accuracy or credibility. Additionally, there is a fear that Generative AI may replace human jobs or lead to biased or unethical outcomes.

To overcome these challenges, businesses must prioritize transparency and education when implementing Generative AI. This includes clearly communicating to users when content has been generated by AI and providing information on how it was created. Additionally, businesses should regularly assess their AI systems for any potential biases and take steps to mitigate them.

Furthermore, building trust with users is crucial for the successful adoption of Generative AI. Businesses should involve users in the development process and gather feedback to continually improve the technology. This will help users feel more comfortable and confident in using Generative AI.

Building User Trust In Generated Outputs

In order to build trust in the generated outputs of Generative AI, businesses must ensure that the quality and accuracy of the content is on par with human-generated content. This can be achieved through rigorous testing and validation processes, as well as investing in skilled data scientists and machine learning experts.

Moreover, it is important for businesses to clearly define the purpose and limitations of their Generative AI systems. This means being transparent about what tasks the technology is best suited for and what it may struggle with. By setting realistic expectations, users will be less likely to doubt or question the output of Generative AI.

Communicating The Capabilities And Limitations Of Generative AI Systems

It is essential for businesses to effectively communicate the capabilities and limitations of their Generative AI systems to users. This means providing clear and concise information on what tasks the technology can perform, how it operates, and what its potential flaws may be.

Additionally, educating users on the ethical considerations surrounding Generative AI can help build trust and understanding. This includes discussing topics such as data privacy, bias, and the potential impact of AI on society. By having open and transparent communication with users, businesses can build a better understanding and acceptance of Generative AI.

Providing User Support And Assistance

As with any new technology, there will be a learning curve for users to become comfortable with Generative AI. To ease this process, businesses should provide user support and assistance. This can include tutorials, FAQs, and access to a customer service team that can address any questions or concerns.

Furthermore, businesses should continually gather feedback from users and use it to improve their Generative AI systems. By implementing updates and addressing common issues, businesses can enhance the user experience and build trust in the technology.

User Education And Engagement Strategies

To fully utilize the potential of Generative AI, users need to be educated and engaged with the technology. Businesses can achieve this by providing resources such as webinars, workshops, and articles that showcase the capabilities and bencfits of Generative AI.

Moreover, businesses need to involve users in the

development process. This can include conducting surveys or focus groups to gather feedback and insight from users. By involving users in the development process, businesses can ensure that their Generative AI systems meet the needs and expectations of their target audience.

Privacy And Security Concerns

The rise of artificial intelligence has presented businesses with a plethora of opportunities and challenges. Generative AI, in particular, offers immense potential for improving efficiency, automating processes and creating innovative solutions. However, one of the major concerns surrounding this technology is privacy and security.

As generative AI systems rely on large amounts of data to learn and generate new content or ideas, there is an inherent risk of sensitive information being exposed or misused. This poses a threat to not only the businesses using generative AI but also their customers and stakeholders.

To overcome these challenges, businesses must prioritize the protection of data privacy and implement robust security measures. This involves implementing strong encryption techniques, regularly updating security protocols, and establishing strict access controls for data.

Moreover, businesses must also educate their employees on the importance of data privacy and security. This includes training staff on best practices for handling sensitive information, such as avoiding sharing login credentials or clicking on suspicious links.

Protecting Sensitive Information In Generated Outputs

Another challenge that businesses face when using generative AI is ensuring that sensitive information does not end up in the outputs generated by these systems. This could include personal data, confidential business information, or proprietary algorithms.

To address this concern, businesses can use techniques such as data masking or differential privacy to ensure that only necessary and non-sensitive information is included in the generated output. They can also conduct regular audits to identify and remove any potential risks of data leakage.

Addressing Privacy Risks In Data Sharing And Model Deployment

In addition to protecting data within their own systems, businesses also need to be cautious when sharing data with third parties or deploying generative AI models. This requires implementing secure data transfer protocols and thoroughly vetting the privacy policies of any partners or vendors that will have access to the data.

Furthermore, businesses should consider using synthetic data instead of real-world data for training generative AI models. Synthetic data is artificially generated and therefore does not contain any personally identifiable information, reducing the risk of privacy breaches.

Overall, protecting sensitive information in the context of generative AI requires a multi-faceted approach that combines encryption techniques, employee education, data masking, secure data transfer protocols, and careful consideration of data sources. By implementing these measures, businesses can harness the power of generative AI while also safeguarding the privacy and confidentiality of their data. Additionally, businesses should regularly review and update their privacy policies and procedures as the landscape of generative AI continues to evolve.

Implementing Robust Security Measures To Prevent Adversarial Attacks

As generative AI becomes more prevalent, the risk of adversarial attacks also increases. Adversarial attacks involve manipulating input data to produce unexpected and potentially harmful results from a generative AI model.

To prevent such attacks, businesses should

implement robust security measures such as anomaly detection systems and strict access controls for their generative AI models. Additionally, regular testing and monitoring of the models can help identify any vulnerabilities and prevent potential attacks.

User Acceptance And Trust

One of the biggest challenges facing businesses when it comes to AI is user acceptance and trust. Many people are skeptical of AI and may view it as a threat to their jobs or privacy. This can lead to resistance and hesitation when it comes to implementing AI solutions in a business setting.

To overcome this challenge, businesses need to focus on transparency and education. Companies need to be transparent about the purpose and capabilities of their AI systems, as well as how they will be used and what data will be collected. This can help build trust with users and alleviate fears of misuse.

In addition, educating employees and customers about AI can also help to increase acceptance and trust. By providing information on how AI works, its potential benefits, and the measures in place to ensure ethical use, businesses can help demystify AI and ease concerns.

Building User Trust In Generated Outputs

Another challenge for businesses using generative

AI is building trust in the outputs it generates. In some cases, people may not be comfortable with the idea of a machine creating something on their behalf. This can be especially true in creative fields such as art or music.

To overcome this challenge, businesses should involve users in the process and give them control over the final result. For example, a user could provide input or feedback on the generated output, allowing them to feel more involved and in control of the final product.

Additionally, businesses can also showcase the capabilities and success of their generative AI systems through case studies or customer testimonials. This can help build trust with potential users and demonstrate the value and reliability of the technology.

Communicating The Capabilities And Limitations Of Generative AI Systems

One of the key ways to build trust with users is to be transparent about the capabilities and limitations of generative AI systems. Businesses should clearly communicate what tasks their AI system can and cannot perform, as well as any potential biases or errors.

This transparency can help manage user expectations and prevent disappointment or mistrust in the technology. It also allows businesses to set boundaries for ethical use and ensure that the AI system is not used for tasks it is not suited for.

User Education And Engagement Strategies

To further build trust and understanding of generative AI, businesses can also invest in user education and engagement strategies. This can include providing resources or tutorials on how the technology works, hosting workshops or events to showcase its capabilities, and actively seeking feedback from users.

By involving users in the process and educating them about generative AI, businesses can not only build trust but also foster a sense of collaboration and partnership with their audience. This can lead to valuable insights and improvements for the technology, as well as stronger relationships with users.

Finance Industry

The finance industry is another sector that has been quick to adopt generative AI. With large amounts of financial data being generated every day, businesses are using generative AI to analyze this data and make better investment decisions. A prime example of this is JPMorgan, which has been using generative AI to analyze financial news and data to identify patterns and make investment recommendations. This has led to improved decision-making and increased profits for the bank.

Another notable example is Goldman Sachs, which has been leveraging generative AI to automate client interactions and provide personalized investment advice. By analyzing customer data, including investment goals and risk tolerance, generative AI algorithms are able to create tailored investment portfolios for each client. This has not only improved the overall customer experience but has also resulted in increased assets under management for the company.

One example of this is J.P. Morgan's use of generative AI in its trading operations. By training a deep learning model on historical trade data, the bank was able to use generative AI to generate highly accurate predictions on future market trends and execute trades accordingly. This resulted in increased efficiency and profitability for the bank's trading desk.

Another case study comes from BlackRock, a global investment management firm. With the help of generative AI, BlackRock was able to improve its risk management processes by generating simulations of potential market scenarios. This allowed the company to identify and mitigate potential risks before they could impact their investments.

In the insurance sector, Allianz has utilized generative AI to transform its claims processing system. By analyzing past claims data, the company's AI system can now generate accurate damage assessments and determine claim payouts in a fraction of the time it took previously. This has not only improved the overall customer experience, but also reduced costs and increased efficiency for the insurance giant.

Examples Of cases In Financial Data

Market Analysis

One example of using generative AI in the financial industry is through market analysis. Through this application, companies are able to use data gathered from various sources and generate insights that can be used to make more informed business decisions.

For instance, a company may collect data on sales revenue, customer demographics, and advertising spending. Using generative AI algorithms, these different pieces of data can be analyzed and combined to provide various insights. These insights may include identifying the most profitable customer segments, determining the effectiveness of different advertising strategies, or predicting future sales trends.

Risk Assessment

Another example of using generative AI in finance is through risk assessment. This application uses machine learning algorithms to analyze large amounts of financial data and identify potential risks that a company may face.

For example, a bank may use generative AI to analyze customer data and identify patterns that could indicate potential credit risks. This can help the bank make more accurate decisions when it comes to approving loans or setting interest rates.

Fraud Detection

Generative AI can also be used for fraud detection in financial transactions. By analyzing large amounts of data and identifying patterns, this technology can help detect any abnormalities or suspicious activities that may indicate fraudulent behavior.

For instance, a credit card company may use generative AI to analyze transaction data and flag any unusual spending patterns. This can help prevent fraud and protect both the company and its customers from financial losses.

Portfolio Optimization

Generative AI can also be used for portfolio optimization in the financial sector. By analyzing market data and historical trends, this technology can help investors make more informed decisions when it comes to creating and managing investment portfolios.

For example, a wealth management firm may use generative AI to analyze stock market data and identify potential investment opportunities that align with their clients' risk profiles and financial goals. This can help maximize returns and minimize risks for both the firm and its clients.

Algorithmic Trading And Market Prediction

Generative AI has also made a significant impact on algorithmic trading and market prediction in the finance industry. By using generative AI algorithms, traders are able to analyze vast amounts of market data and make predictions about future trends with greater accuracy. This has led to increased profits for investment firms and hedge funds, as well as reduced risk in their trading strategies.

One notable example is the hedge fund Renaissance Technologies, which uses generative AI algorithms to analyze financial markets and make investment decisions. This has allowed the company to consistently outperform traditional trading methods and generate exceptionally high returns for its investors.

Generative AI For Predictive Modeling In Trading

Generative AI has also revolutionized predictive modeling in trading, allowing traders to forecast future market trends and make more informed investment decisions. By analyzing historical data and using generative AI algorithms, traders are able to identify patterns and trends that may not be visible to the human eye. This has allowed them to make more accurate predictions about stock prices, currency exchange rates, and other market fluctuations.

Generative AI has also been used in risk management and portfolio optimization for trading firms. By analyzing different scenarios and potential outcomes, generative AI algorithms can assist traders in making more informed decisions about their investment strategies. This has reduced the overall risk in trading activities and led to more successful trades.

Customer Personalization And Recommendation Systems

One of the most popular use cases for generative AI in business is customer personalization and recommendation systems. These systems use machine learning algorithms to analyze data on customers' past behaviors, preferences and interests, and then generate personalized recommendations for products or services that are likely to be of interest to each individual customer.

This type of generative AI has become increasingly important for businesses as competition in various industries has grown, and customers have become more demanding for personalized experiences. Companies that invest in generative AI for customer personalization and recommendation systems are able to improve customer engagement, increase sales and revenue, and ultimately build stronger relationships with their customers.

Moreover, generative AI can also be used to create personalized marketing content that is tailored specifically to each individual customer. This has a significant impact on the effectiveness of marketing campaigns and has been shown to increase conversion rates significantly.

CHAPTER 8: MARKETING AND ADVERTISING

Generative AI, in particular, has caught the attention of many business owners and marketers due to its ability to create unique and creative content on a large scale. With generative AI, businesses can automate the process of content creation and improve their overall marketing and advertising strategies.

How Can Generative AI Benefit Marketing And Advertising?

1. Cost-Effective: With traditional marketing and advertising, businesses often have to invest a significant amount of time and money in creating and promoting content. Generative AI can significantly reduce this cost by automating the process, allowing businesses to create more content in less time.
2. Scalability: Another advantage of generative AI is its scalability. It can generate a large number of variations of content, making it easier for businesses to target different segments and increase their reach.
3. Creativity Boost: Generative AI uses machine learning algorithms to analyze

existing content and come up with unique ideas and variations. This not only saves time but also sparks creativity, allowing businesses to come up with more innovative and engaging content.
4. Faster Turnaround: In the fast-paced world of marketing and advertising, speed is crucial. With generative AI, businesses can create content at a much faster pace, allowing them to stay ahead of their competitors.
5. Constantly Evolving: Generative AI continuously learns and evolves based on the feedback it receives. This means that the more content it creates, the more accurate and effective it becomes in generating quality content.
6. Multilingual Capabilities: With global markets becoming increasingly important for businesses, generative AI can help by creating multilingual content in different languages, making it easier to connect with a wider audience.
7. Data-Driven Insights: Generative AI collects and analyzes data from various sources to generate content. This provides businesses with valuable insights into their target audience, allowing them to create more targeted and effective campaigns.
8. Personalization: By analyzing user

behavior and preferences, generative AI can personalize content for different individuals or groups, making it more relevant and engaging for the audience.
9. Versatility: Generative AI can be used in various forms of content creation, including written, visual, and audio. This versatility makes it a valuable tool for businesses looking to create diverse and impactful content.
10. Integration with other tools: Generative AI can be integrated with other marketing tools such as social media management platforms or email marketing software, making it easier for businesses to streamline their content creation process.
11. Reduced Costs: With generative AI, businesses can reduce their content creation costs by eliminating the need for manual labor or outsourcing to external agencies. This saves both time and money, allowing businesses to allocate resources towards other important areas.

Traditional Approaches vs. Modern Trends:

Traditional marketing and advertising strategies have been around for decades and are still widely used by businesses today. These include methods such as print ads, television commercials, and billboards. However, with the rise of technology and the internet, new forms of marketing and advertising have emerged.

One of these modern trends is generative AI. Generative AI refers to the use of artificial intelligence to generate content, such as images, text, or videos. This technology has the potential to revolutionize the way businesses approach their marketing and advertising strategies.

Personalization and Targeting:

One of the biggest advantages of using generative AI in marketing and advertising is its ability to personalize content for individual consumers. With traditional methods, a single ad or message is shown to a large audience, regardless of their specific interests or preferences. This often leads to a low conversion rate as not everyone will be interested in the product or service being advertised.

Generative AI, on the other hand, can analyze data and create personalized content for each individual based on their online behavior, demographics, and other factors. This can result in higher engagement and conversion rates as the content is tailored to the specific interests of each consumer.

Enhanced Creativity:

Another benefit of using generative AI in marketing and advertising is its ability to enhance creativity. Traditional methods often rely on human creativity and can be limited by budget constraints and time limitations. Generative AI, on the other hand, can generate an endless amount of content, making it easier for businesses to experiment with different ideas and concepts without any additional costs.

Types Of AI In Marketing And Advertising

1. **Natural Language Processing (NLP):** This type of AI uses algorithms to understand and analyze human language. In marketing and advertising, NLP can be used to create more effective targeted ads by analyzing consumer behavior and sentiment.
2. **Machine Learning:** Machine learning is a form of AI that allows computers to learn from data without being explicitly programmed. This can be applied to marketing and advertising by analyzing large amounts of consumer data to identify patterns and predict future behaviors.
3. **Computer Vision:** This type of AI uses image recognition and object detection algorithms to understand visual content. In marketing and advertising, computer vision can be used for tasks such as product recognition in images or video content.
4. **Chatbots/Virtual Assistants:** Chatbots

and virtual assistants use natural language processing and machine learning to interact with users in a conversational manner. In marketing and advertising, these AI tools can be used for customer service, lead generation, and personalized product recommendations.
5. **Generative Adversarial Networks (GANs):** GANs are a type of deep learning that uses two neural networks – one to generate new content and one to discriminate between generated and real content. In marketing and advertising, GANs can be used to create realistic images or videos for product campaigns.

How AI Is Revolutionizing Marketing And Advertising

AI has revolutionized the way businesses advertise and market their products or services. Here are some ways that AI is changing the game in marketing and advertising:

1. **Personalization:** With AI, businesses can gather and analyze vast amounts of consumer data to create more personalized and targeted ads. This means that instead of showing the same generic ad to all viewers, AI can help identify specific target audiences and tailor ads to their interests and behaviors.

2. **Improved Targeting:** By using machine learning algorithms, businesses can better understand their target audience's behavior and sentiment. This allows them to create more effective ad campaigns that are targeted toward the right audience at the right time.
3. **Real-time Optimization:** AI-powered tools can analyze consumer data in real-time and make necessary adjustments to ad campaigns to improve their performance. This means businesses can save time and resources by automatically optimizing their ads instead of manually analyzing data and making changes.
4. **Efficiency:** AI-powered chatbots are being used to streamline customer service processes and handle repetitive tasks such as answering frequently asked questions. This allows businesses to provide faster and more efficient customer service, freeing up time for employees to focus on higher-value tasks.
5. **Lead Generation:** AI can help identify potential customers by analyzing their online behavior, interests, and social media interactions. This allows businesses to target specific individuals or groups who are most likely to be interested in their products or services, increasing the likelihood of lead

conversion.
6. **Predictive Analytics:** AI-powered tools can analyze consumer data and predict future trends and behaviors. This allows businesses to anticipate customer needs and preferences, enabling them to create more targeted and effective ad campaigns.
7. **Hyper-personalization:** With AI, businesses can create highly personalized and targeted ads that resonate with each individual consumer. This level of personalization can lead to higher engagement rates and conversions.
8. **Cost Savings:** By automating tasks and processes, AI can help businesses save time and money on labor costs. With efficient ad targeting and optimization, businesses can also reduce their ad spend while still achieving better results.

AI Applications In Advertising:

One of the most promising applications of AI in advertising is personalization. With AI algorithms, businesses can now create highly targeted and customized advertisements based on an individual's interests, behavior, and preferences. This level of personalization allows companies to deliver more relevant and engaging ads, increasing the chances of conversion.

AI is also being used to improve ad placement by analyzing consumer data and identifying the most effective channels for reaching a specific target audience. This not only helps businesses save money by avoiding ad placements that are unlikely to generate results but also improves the overall customer experience by ensuring ads are shown in the right place at the right time.

In addition, AI is being used for content creation and optimization. By analyzing consumer data, AI algorithms can identify which types of content perform best with different target audiences. This allows businesses to create more effective and engaging ads that resonate with their target market.

Ad Creativity And Design:

AI is also being used to enhance the creativity and design of advertisements. With AI-powered tools, businesses can now automate certain aspects of ad creation such as image selection, copywriting, and layout design. This not only saves time and resources but also allows for more experimentation and refinement in the creative process.

Moreover, AI can assist in generating new ideas for ads by analyzing consumer behavior, interests, and trends. This can help businesses come up with unique and innovative ad concepts that are more likely to capture the attention of their target audience.

In the future, AI is expected to play an even bigger role in advertising as it continues to evolve and improve. With advancements in natural language processing (NLP) and machine learning (ML), AI will be able to understand and interpret human language and behavior more accurately. This will enable businesses to create highly personalized ads that cater to individual preferences and needs.

Ad Copywriting And Optimization:

AI is also revolutionizing the way ad copywriting and optimization are done. By analyzing data and consumer behavior, AI algorithms can suggest the most effective words, phrases, and call-to-actions to use in ad copy. This helps businesses craft more persuasive and compelling messages that drive higher conversions.

In addition, AI can continuously monitor and analyze ad performance in real-time, making automatic adjustments to optimize ad campaigns for better results. This eliminates the need for manual monitoring and testing, allowing businesses to allocate their resources more efficiently.

Ad Placement Optimization:

AI can also assist in optimizing ad placement for maximum impact. By analyzing user data, AI algorithms can determine the most relevant and high-performing ad placements on different platforms and devices. This allows businesses to target their ads more effectively, resulting in higher click-through rates and conversions.

In addition, AI can help businesses identify the best times to display their ads based on user behavior and engagement patterns. This ensures that ads are shown at the most opportune moments when they are most likely to grab the audience's attention.

Ad Performance Prediction:

With the help of machine learning algorithms, AI can predict ad performance and outcomes based on historical data. This allows businesses to make more informed decisions when creating and optimizing ad campaigns, resulting in better ROI.

Moreover, AI can also identify potential issues or negative trends in ad performance before they become significant problems. This helps businesses mitigate risks and make proactive adjustments to their ad strategies for better results.

Fraud Detection:

Advertising fraud is a major concern for businesses, as it can significantly impact ad performance and budget. AI-powered tools can detect and prevent fraudulent activities such as click farms, bot traffic, and fake leads.

By continuously monitoring for suspicious activity and using anomaly detection techniques, AI can help eliminate advertising fraud, ensuring that businesses are getting accurate data and maximizing the effectiveness of their ad campaigns.

Personalization:

AI can also aid in creating personalized ads that are tailored to each individual user. By analyzing user behavior and preferences, AI algorithms can deliver targeted ad content that resonates with the audience and increases engagement.

This personalization not only improves ad performance but also enhances the overall customer experience, leading to increased brand loyalty and customer retention.

A/B Testing:

A/B testing is a critical part of ad performance optimization, as it allows businesses to compare different versions of an ad and determine which one performs better. However, manually conducting A/B tests can be time-consuming and resource-intensive.

With the help of AI algorithms, businesses can automate the process of A/B testing and quickly identify the most effective version of an ad, saving time and resources while improving overall performance.

Challenges Of Generative AI For Marketing And Advertising

1. Generating Content With High Quality

One of the main challenges of generative AI for marketing and advertising is generating content with high quality. In today's digital age, content is king, and businesses need to produce high-quality and engaging content regularly to attract and retain customers. Generating this type of content can be time-consuming and resource-intensive for businesses.

However, with the help of generative AI, businesses can automate the content creation process and produce high-quality content at a faster rate. The challenge here is to train the AI model to understand what constitutes as high-quality and engaging content for the target audience.

2. Personalization and Targeting

Another challenge of using generative AI for marketing and advertising is personalization and targeting. With traditional methods, businesses have to manually gather customer data and create targeted campaigns. With generative AI, this process can be automated, but the challenge lies in training the model to understand customer preferences and behavior accurately.

Moreover, personalization is not just limited to

content creation but also extends to ad targeting. Businesses need to ensure that their ads are shown to the right audience at the right time, and with the help of generative AI, this can be achieved. However, it requires constant testing and tweaking to ensure accurate targeting.

3. Balance Between Automation And Human Creativity

Generative AI for marketing and advertising aims to automate the content creation process. Still, there is a need for human creativity in developing impactful campaigns. Striking the right balance between automation and human creativity is a challenge that businesses face in incorporating generative AI into their marketing strategies.

While AI can come up with new ideas and generate content, it lacks the emotional intelligence and understanding of human behavior. This makes it essential for businesses to have a creative team that can work alongside the AI model to produce truly engaging and personalized content.

4. Ethical Considerations

As with any technology, there are ethical considerations that come into play when using generative AI for marketing and advertising. The use of customer data raises concerns about privacy and consumer protection. Businesses must be transparent with their customers about the use of AI in their marketing strategies and ensure that their data is handled ethically.

Additionally, there is a risk of perpetuating bias and reinforcing stereotypes in the content generated by AI. To prevent this, it is crucial to have a diverse team that can provide different perspectives and inputs when training the AI model.

5.The Future of Marketing with Generative AI

Despite its potential drawbacks, generative AI holds immense promise for the future of marketing and advertising. As technology continues to advance, we can expect to see more sophisticated AI models that can produce even more personalized and compelling content.

Moreover, businesses must adapt to the changing landscape of marketing and embrace the use of AI to stay competitive. By leveraging generative AI, companies can streamline their content creation process, improve customer engagement, and drive sales.

Real-world Examples Of Generative AI Implementation In Marketing And Advertising

Some companies that have already implemented generative AI in their marketing and advertising strategies include:

1. **Adobe Spark**: Adobe Spark is a popular design tool that uses generative AI to create professional-looking designs

in just a few clicks. This has been particularly useful for small businesses and marketers who may not have the resources to hire professional designers.

2. **Pepsi**: In 2019, Pepsi launched a campaign that used generative AI to create over 200 unique and personalized video ads. This helped the company reach a wider audience and increase engagement with their brand.

3. **Netflix**: Netflix uses generative AI to personalize its movie recommendations for each user based on their viewing history. This has led to an increase in user retention and engagement on the platform.

4. **Burger King**: Burger King launched a campaign in Brazil that used generative AI to create over 50,000 unique posters for their restaurants. This helped them stand out among their competition and attract more customers.

5. **L'Oreal**: L'Oreal uses generative AI to personalize their advertisements for different regions and demographics. This has helped them increase their reach and connect with their target audience effectively.

6. **IBM Watson**: IBM Watson has been used by many companies in the marketing and advertising industry to analyze

customer data, predict trends, and create targeted campaigns using generative AI technology.

7. **Pandora**: Pandora uses generative AI to create personalized playlists for its users based on their listening habits and preferences. This has led to an increase in user satisfaction and retention on the music streaming platform.
8. **Sephora**: Sephora uses generative AI to offer personalized beauty recommendations and virtual try-on experiences for their customers online. This has improved the shopping experience for their customers and increased sales for the company.
9. **Google**: Google uses generative AI to improve its search engine algorithms, making it easier for users to find relevant and personalized results. This has led to an increase in user satisfaction and loyalty towards the search engine giant.
10. **Nike**: Nike uses generative AI to design and create personalized shoes for their customers. This has not only improved the customer experience but also allowed Nike to stay ahead of trends and offer unique products in the highly competitive sports industry.

CHAPTER 9 : GENERATIVE AI IN TRADING

Generative AI in Trading is an emerging technology that is revolutionizing the way financial markets operate. It combines artificial intelligence (AI) and machine learning (ML) techniques to generate predictive models of market behavior and trends.

This technology has gained significant traction in recent years due to its ability to process vast amounts of data, extract insights, and make accurate predictions in real-time. As a result, it has become an invaluable tool for traders, financial analysts, and investment firms in making critical trading decisions.

Benefits Of Generative AI In Trading

Generative AI offers several advantages over traditional trading methods, including:

1. **Efficiency:** By leveraging advanced algorithms and machine learning techniques, generative AI can analyze vast amounts of data at high speeds. This allows traders to make more informed decisions in a fraction of the time it would take with traditional methods.
2. **Accuracy:** Generative AI models continually learn and improve from new

data, making accurate predictions and identifying patterns that humans may not be able to detect. This can give traders a competitive edge in the market and increase their chances of success.

3. **Automation:** With generative AI, traders can automate several routine tasks, such as data analysis and market monitoring. This frees up their time to focus on more critical activities, such as strategy development and risk management.
4. **Risk Management:** Generative AI can help traders manage risk by identifying potential market fluctuations or anomalies in real-time. This allows them to make informed decisions and minimize losses.

Traditional Trading Approaches vs. Generative AI

While traditional trading approaches rely on human analysis and intuition, generative AI uses quantitative data-driven strategies to make predictions and decisions.

Traditional trading methods also have limitations in terms of processing large amounts of data, identifying patterns, and detecting market trends accurately. This is where generative AI provides a significant advantage by leveraging advanced algorithms and machine learning techniques to analyze vast amounts of data and identify complex patterns and relationships.

Moreover, traditional trading approaches can be influenced by human emotions such as fear and greed, which can lead to biased decision-making. Generative AI eliminates this risk by making objective decisions based on data analysis.

Automated execution is another area where generative AI outperforms traditional trading methods. While humans may make mistakes or miss out on profitable opportunities, generative AI can execute trades at lightning speed and with high accuracy.

In addition to these advantages, generative AI also offers more comprehensive risk management capabilities. By constantly monitoring market trends and anomalies, it can help traders make timely decisions to minimize losses and maximize profits.

Role of Data In Financial Markets

Data plays a crucial role in financial markets as it is the foundation of all trading decisions. Without data, traders would have no information to base their strategies and decisions on.

In traditional trading approaches, data was limited to historical market data and indicators such as moving averages and trend lines. However, with the rise of generative AI, the amount and variety of data used in trading have increased significantly.

Generative AI relies on various types of data, including market data such as stock prices and economic indicators, news and social media sentiment, and even alternative data sources like satellite imagery and credit card transactions. By analyzing a diverse range of data, generative AI can provide more accurate insights into market trends and behaviors.

Moreover, the speed at which generative AI can process and analyze large volumes of data gives it a significant advantage over traditional trading methods. In the fast-paced financial markets, having access to real-time data and insights is crucial for making profitable trades.

Potential Impact On Financial Markets

The adoption of generative AI in financial markets has the potential to revolutionize the industry. Its ability to make unbiased, data-driven decisions can help minimize human error and emotions, which are often the downfall of traders.

Furthermore, generative AI has the potential to level the playing field for smaller investors by providing them with access to advanced data analysis tools that were previously only available to large financial institutions. This democratization of data could lead to a more fair and efficient market.

However, there are also concerns about the potential impact of generative AI on financial markets. Some fear that the use of AI and automation could lead to a loss of jobs in the industry, particularly for traders and analysts.

Moreover, there are also ethical concerns surrounding the use of generative AI in trading. As with any technology, there is always a risk of bias or manipulation in the data used to train these systems. If not monitored and regulated carefully, generative AI could perpetuate existing inequalities in the financial markets.

Types Of AI In Trading

Trading is an industry that involves buying and selling financial assets such as stocks, commodities, or currencies. With the advancement of technology, trading has become more efficient and precise. One of the major developments in the field of trading is the use of Artificial Intelligence (AI) techniques to analyze market data and make predictions about future trends.

There are different types of AI used in trading, and one of them is Generative AI. Generative AI uses algorithms to create new data based on the patterns and trends found in existing data. This type of AI has become increasingly popular in trading due to its ability to generate more accurate predictions compared to traditional statistical models.

Applications Of Generative AI In Trading

1. **Risk Management**: One of the key applications of generative AI in trading is risk management. This technology can analyze large amounts of market data and identify potential risks, allowing traders to make better-informed decisions.
2. **Pattern Recognition**: Generative AI can also be used for pattern recognition, which is crucial for successful trading. By analyzing historical data, this technology can identify patterns and trends that have the potential to repeat in the future.
3. **Algorithmic Trading**: With the use of generative AI, trading algorithms can be created that make real-time decisions based on market conditions. This not only speeds up the trading process but also reduces human errors and emotions.
4. **Portfolio Optimization**: Generative AI can also assist traders in optimizing their portfolios by using predictive modeling to determine the best allocation of assets. This can help minimize risk and maximize returns.
5. **Market Analysis**: Another important application of generative AI in trading is market analysis. By analyzing vast amounts of data from various sources,

this technology can provide insights into market trends, sentiments, and potential opportunities for traders to capitalize on.
6. **High-Frequency Trading**: Generative AI has also revolutionized high-frequency trading, where large volumes of trades are executed within milliseconds. This technology can analyze market data and make split-second decisions, allowing traders to take advantage of small price discrepancies.
7. **Sentiment Analysis**: By using natural language processing (NLP) techniques, generative AI can analyze news articles, social media posts, and other sources to determine market sentiment. This information can be valuable for traders to make informed decisions.
8. **Market Forecasting**: By analyzing historical data and using predictive modeling, generative AI can forecast future market movements with a high degree of accuracy. This can help traders make better-informed decisions and stay ahead of the competition.

Concepts And Techniques Used in Generative AI

1. **Machine Learning**: Generative AI uses machine learning algorithms to analyze large amounts of data and learn patterns and relationships between variables.

2. **Natural Language Processing (NLP)**: This technique is used to process and analyze natural language data, such as news articles, social media posts, and other sources of textual data.
3. **Deep Learning**: This technique involves training neural networks with large amounts of data to learn and make predictions on new data.
4. **Reinforcement Learning**: Generative AI also utilizes reinforcement learning, where algorithms are trained to make decisions and improve their performance based on feedback from the environment.
5. **Predictive Modeling**: Predictive modeling involves using statistical techniques and machine learning algorithms to forecast future outcomes based on historical data.
6. **Data Mining**: Generative AI relies heavily on data mining, which involves identifying and extracting patterns and insights from large datasets.
7. **Simulation**: Simulation techniques are used to create virtual environments that mimic real-world scenarios, allowing generative AI algorithms to learn and make predictions in a controlled setting.
8. **Natural Language Generation (NLG)**: NLG is a subfield of NLP that focuses on generating human-like text based on data inputs.

9. **Computer Vision**: This technique involves using algorithms to recognize and interpret visual data, such as images and videos.
10. **Probabilistic Graphical Models**: These models are used in generative AI to represent complex relationships between variables and make probabilistic predictions.
11. **Collaborative Filtering**: This technique is commonly used in recommendation systems, where algorithms learn from user behavior and make personalized suggestions.

Sentiment Analysis And News Generation

Sentiment analysis is another area where generative AI has shown great potential. This involves using algorithms to analyze text data and determine the overall sentiment or emotion behind it. It can be used for various purposes such as understanding customer feedback, predicting stock market trends, and monitoring social media sentiment.

News generation is another emerging application of generative AI. With the increasing demand for real-time news updates, traditional media outlets are turning to AI algorithms to automatically generate news articles. These algorithms use natural language processing and machine learning techniques to analyze data from various sources and generate coherent and relevant news stories.

Generative AI has also paved the way for deepfakes, which are images or videos that have been doctored using AI algorithms. While this technology has raised concerns about its potential misuse, it also has potential applications such as creating more realistic video game graphics and improving special effects in movies.

High-Frequency Trading And Market Making

High-frequency trading (HFT) and market making are two other areas where generative AI is being used. HFT involves using algorithms to make high-speed trades in financial markets, based on real-time data and market trends. This allows for more efficient trading and can lead to higher profits.

Market making refers to the practice of continuously buying and selling securities in order to provide liquidity in the market. Generative AI algorithms can help with this by analyzing large amounts of data and making quick decisions on when to buy or sell, thus optimizing market making strategies.

Liquidity Provisioning

In addition to market making, generative AI is also being used for liquidity provisioning. This involves creating a constant supply of assets or currencies in the market in order to maintain stability and prevent price fluctuations. Generative AI algorithms can analyze market data and make real-time decisions on when and how much liquidity to provide.

Challenges Of Generative AI In Trading

Generative AI solutions in trading face various challenges that make it difficult for efficient use and adoption. These challenges can be broadly categorized into the following:

Data Availability:

The biggest challenge of generative AI in trading is the availability of quality data. Trading involves working with large amounts of historical market data, which may not always be readily available or easily accessible. Moreover, the data may also be incomplete or have errors, making it difficult for generative AI models to accurately learn and make predictions. This poses a major challenge for traders who are looking to use generative AI in their trading strategies.

Data Quality:

In addition to data availability, the quality of the data also plays a crucial role in the performance of generative AI models. Poor quality data can lead to inaccurate predictions and ultimately result in losses for traders. This is why it is important for traders to ensure that the data they use for generative AI models is accurate, clean, and reliable.

Interpretability:

Generative AI models are often seen as "black boxes" which make it challenging for traders to interpret the decisions or predictions made by these models. This lack of interpretability can be a major hindrance for traders who need to understand the reasoning behind a model's predictions in order to make informed decisions.

Overfitting:

Another major challenge faced by generative AI models in trading is overfitting. Overfitting occurs when a model performs well on training data but poorly on unseen or new data. In trading, this can lead to the model making inaccurate predictions based on historical data that may not accurately reflect the current market conditions. Traders must carefully train their generative AI models to avoid overfitting and ensure that it is able to adapt to changing market conditions.

Integration:

Integrating generative AI into existing trading systems can also be a challenge for traders. This requires a thorough understanding of both generative AI and trading systems, as well as the ability to effectively combine them in a seamless manner. Traders may also need to consider potential conflicts between the AI model and existing strategies or risk management protocols.

Human Oversight:

Despite the advancements in generative AI technology, human oversight is still necessary for successful implementation in trading. This includes monitoring and evaluating the performance of the AI model, as well as making adjustments or overrides when necessary. Human intervention is also crucial for addressing any ethical concerns that may arise from using generative AI in trading.

Future Directions:

Despite the challenges mentioned above, there is a growing interest in using generative AI models in trading due to their potential to improve decision-making and increase profitability. In the future, we can expect to see further advancements in this field as technology continues to evolve and more data becomes available for training these models. Additionally, research into ethical implications and regulations surrounding the use of generative AI in trading will also continue to be an important area of focus. As such, traders should keep a close eye on developments in generative AI and consider incorporating it into their trading strategies as the technology continues to mature. With proper implementation and monitoring, generative AI has the potential to revolutionize the world of trading and help traders stay ahead in an increasingly complex market. Overall, the future looks bright for generative AI in trading, and its role in decision-making is only expected to increase over time.

Real-world Examples Of Generative AI Implementation In Trading

In the world of financial markets, trading is a highly competitive and dynamic field where every second counts. Traders are always on the lookout for new tools and technologies that can give them an edge in making profitable trades. In recent years, generative AI has emerged as one such technology that has caught the attention of traders.

Generative AI uses deep learning algorithms to generate new data based on patterns and relationships in existing data. This can be extremely useful in trading as it can analyze large volumes of historical market data and identify potential future trends or patterns that can help traders make more informed decisions.

One area where generative AI has been successfully implemented is in automated trading systems. These are computer programs that use predefined rules and algorithms to automatically execute trades without human intervention. Generative AI can help improve the accuracy of these algorithms by continuously generating and updating data, leading to better trading decisions.

Another example is in the prediction and forecasting of market trends. Generative AI models can analyze vast amounts of data from different sources such as news articles, social media, and economic reports to make predictions about future price movements. This information can be valuable for traders to adjust their strategies and make more informed trades.

Moreover, generative AI can also aid in risk management. By continuously analyzing market data, it can identify potential risks and anomalies in real-time, allowing traders to take proactive measures to mitigate them. This is particularly useful in high-frequency trading, where even the slightest changes in the market can have a significant impact on profits or losses.

In addition to these applications, generative AI is also being used in sentiment analysis. By analyzing text data from various sources, it can gauge the overall sentiment towards a particular asset or market, providing traders with valuable insights into potential market movements.

CHAPTER 10 : GENERATIVE AI AND MACHINE LEARNING

Machine Learning

Machine Learning is a subset of Artificial Intelligence (AI) that deals with teaching computers to learn from data without explicitly programming them. This means that machine learning algorithms can automatically identify patterns in data and make decisions based on those patterns.

There are different types of Machine Learning, the most popular ones being: supervised learning, unsupervised learning, semi-supervised learning, and reinforcement learning.

Supervised Learning: In this type of Machine Learning, the algorithm is provided with a set of labeled data. The algorithm learns from these labels and creates a model that can predict outcomes for new, unseen data. This type of learning is commonly used in tasks such as image recognition, speech recognition, and natural language processing.

Unsupervised Learning: As opposed to supervised learning, unsupervised learning doesn't use labeled data. Instead, the algorithm looks for patterns and relationships within the data on its own. This type of learning is useful in tasks such as clustering and anomaly detection.

Semi-Supervised Learning: This type of learning combines elements from both supervised and unsupervised learning. It uses a small amount of labeled data along with a larger amount of unlabeled data to train the algorithm. This can be helpful when there is a limited availability of labeled data.

Reinforcement Learning: Reinforcement learning involves training an algorithm to make decisions based on rewards and punishments. The algorithm learns through trial and error, receiving positive reinforcement for correct actions and negative reinforcement for incorrect actions.

Machine learning has many applications in various fields such as healthcare, finance, and marketing. Some common applications include:

1. Predictive analytics: This involves using machine learning algorithms to forecast future trends based on historical data.
2. Fraud detection: Machine learning algorithms can be used to detect fraudulent activities by identifying patterns in data.
3. Recommendation systems: These systems use machine learning algorithms to suggest products or services to users based on their past behavior and

preferences.
4. Natural language processing: This involves using machine learning to understand and analyze human language, enabling applications such as chatbots and voice assistants.

Predictive Analytics

Predictive analytics is the practice of using data, statistical algorithms and machine learning techniques to identify the likelihood of future outcomes based on historical data. This can be used in various fields such as marketing, finance, healthcare, and more.

Some common predictive analytics techniques include regression analysis, time series forecasting, and decision trees. These techniques help to make accurate predictions by analyzing patterns and relationships within data.

Predictive analytics has many benefits, including:

1. Anticipating and mitigating risks: By predicting future outcomes, organizations can identify potential risks and take proactive measures to mitigate them.
2. Improving decision-making: Predictive analytics provides valuable insights based on data analysis, helping organizations make informed decisions.

3. Enhancing customer experience: By understanding customer behavior and preferences, organizations can tailor their products and services to meet their needs.
4. Increasing efficiency and productivity: Predictive analytics can optimize processes by identifying inefficiencies and suggesting improvements.

With the increasing availability of data and advancements in machine learning technology, predictive analytics is becoming more accurate and valuable for businesses. It allows organizations to stay ahead of the competition by making data-driven decisions and predicting future trends.

Challenges Of Predictive Analytics

While predictive analytics has many benefits, it also comes with some challenges. Some of the common challenges include:

1. Data quality and availability: Predictive analytics is heavily reliant on data. If the data is messy or incomplete, it can affect the accuracy of predictions.
2. Selection bias: The algorithms used in predictive analytics are based on historical data, which can lead to bias if the data is not representative of the entire population.
3. Interpretation and communication:

Predictive analytics outputs can be complex and difficult to understand for non-technical stakeholders. Communicating the results effectively is crucial for gaining buy-in and implementing changes based on the predictions.

Fraud detection

Fraud detection is an essential task for any business. Fraudulent activities can result in significant financial loss, legal troubles, and damage to the company's reputation. With the rise of online transactions and digital payments, fraud detection has become more challenging as criminals find new ways to exploit loopholes in systems.

Generative AI and machine learning techniques have proven to be useful tools in fraud detection. These techniques involve training algorithms on large datasets to detect patterns and anomalies in transactions, which can help identify potentially fraudulent activities.

One such example is the use of generative adversarial networks (GANs) in detecting credit card fraud. GANs are a type of generative AI model that uses two neural networks, one to generate data and the other to discriminate between real and fake data. By training the discriminator network on a large dataset of legitimate credit card transactions, it can learn to detect abnormal or fraudulent transactions.

Recommendation Systems

Recommendation systems have become an integral part of many businesses, especially in the e-commerce industry. These systems use generative AI and machine learning techniques to analyze customer data and provide personalized recommendations.

One popular approach is collaborative filtering, where algorithms are trained on a user's past behavior and preferences as well as other users' similar behaviors to recommend products or services that the user may be interested in. This method has proven to be highly effective, with companies like Amazon and Netflix using it to provide personalized recommendations to their customers.

Another approach is content-based filtering, where algorithms analyze the attributes of products or services that a customer has previously interacted with and recommend similar items. For example, if a customer frequently purchases clothing items from an online store, the system may recommend other clothing items with similar styles, sizes, or brands.

In addition to these methods, hybrid recommendation systems combine multiple techniques to provide more accurate and diverse recommendations. These systems can use a combination of collaborative filtering, content-based filtering, and even demographic information to further personalize recommendations for users.

Fraud Detection And Recommendation Systems

While fraud detection and recommendation systems may seem like completely different applications of AI and machine learning, they share some similarities in their underlying techniques. Both rely on analyzing large amounts of data and using advanced algorithms to make accurate predictions.

In the case of fraud detection, algorithms are trained to detect patterns and anomalies in financial transactions that may indicate fraudulent activity. This is similar to recommendation systems, where algorithms analyze past behaviors and preferences to make predictions about what a user may be interested in.

Moreover, both fraud detection and recommendation systems require constant updates and improvements to stay effective. As technology advances and new methods of fraud emerge, algorithms must continuously learn and adapt to detect these new patterns. Similarly, recommendation systems need to consider shifts in consumer behavior and preferences to provide relevant recommendations.

In many cases, companies use the same technology for both fraud detection and recommendation systems, leveraging the similarities in their techniques. This not only streamlines processes and saves resources but also allows for a more comprehensive understanding of consumer behavior.

With the rise of e-commerce and online shopping, fraud detection has become increasingly important for protecting consumers and businesses alike. Recommendation systems have also become essential tools for companies looking to improve customer satisfaction and increase sales. As these technologies continue to evolve and improve, their impact on industries such as retail, finance, and marketing will only become more significant.

In the future, we may see even more overlap between fraud detection and recommendation systems as companies look for ways to use AI and machine learning to enhance both processes. For example, some companies are exploring the possibility of using recommendation systems to identify patterns of fraud in large datasets. By leveraging the power of AI, companies can not only improve their fraud detection but also provide more personalized and accurate recommendations for their customers.

Natural Language Processing (NLP)

Generative AI is a subset of artificial intelligence that deals with generating new data or content based on patterns and input data. It is also known as creative AI because it mimics the human ability to create, imagine and learn. Generative AI uses techniques such as machine learning, deep learning, and natural language processing (NLP) to generate new text, images, videos, and even music.

NLP is a field of artificial intelligence that enables machines to understand, interpret and process human language. It involves teaching computers how to analyze and extract meaning from human speech and text data. NLP is the backbone of generative AI as it allows machines to learn patterns from existing text data and generate new content based on those patterns.

Personalized Customer Interactions

Generative AI has the potential to revolutionize customer interactions in business. By analyzing large amounts of customer data, generative AI can create personalized responses and recommendations for each individual customer. This not only enhances the customer experience but also improves customer engagement and retention.

For example, imagine a chatbot that uses generative AI to have natural conversations with customers, understanding their needs and preferences, and providing personalized solutions in real-time. This not only saves time for the customer but also increases their satisfaction with the brand. Additionally, generative AI can also be used to generate personalized product recommendations for customers based on their previous purchases and browsing history.

Applications Of Generative AI In Machine Learning

Generative AI has shown immense potential in the field of machine learning, especially in tasks that require creativity and intuition. Some of the key applications of generative AI in machine learning include:

1) Image Generation: One of the most well-known applications of generative AI is image generation. This involves creating new images from scratch using deep learning algorithms. Generative adversarial networks (GANs) have been used to generate realistic images that are almost indistinguishable from real ones.

2) Text Generation: Generative AI has also been used to create text, such as articles, stories, and even code. This is often achieved by feeding large amounts of data into a neural network and training it to generate new content based on the patterns it learns from the data.

3) Music Generation: Another creative application

of generative AI is music generation. With the use of recurrent neural networks (RNNs), generative AI can create new melodies and songs based on existing music data.

4) Video Generation: Similar to image generation, generative AI can be used to generate videos by predicting future frames based on previous ones. This is often used in video processing and animation.

5) Data Augmentation: Generative AI can also be used for data augmentation, a technique commonly used in machine learning to increase the amount of training data. This helps improve the performance of models by providing more diverse data to learn from.

6) Chatbots and Virtual Assistants: Generative AI has also been used to create chatbots and virtual assistants that can interact with users in a conversational manner. These AI-powered assistants are becoming increasingly common in various industries, such as customer service and healthcare.

Business Leaders And Machine Learning:

Machine Learning and Artificial Intelligence have become buzzwords in the business world, with many companies incorporating these technologies into their operations. These cutting-edge technologies are transforming businesses and giving them a competitive edge. Business leaders need to understand the potential of Machine Learning and how it can benefit their organizations.

One of the main advantages of Machine Learning is its ability to analyze large amounts of data quickly and accurately. This is particularly useful in business decision-making processes, as it can help identify patterns and trends that humans may not be able to detect. Machine Learning algorithms can also continuously learn from new data, making them more accurate and efficient over time.

With the use of Machine Learning, businesses can automate tedious and repetitive tasks, allowing employees to focus on more complex and strategic work. This can lead to increased productivity and cost savings for the organization. Additionally, Machine Learning can help businesses improve their customer service by analyzing customer data and providing personalized recommendations.

Another major benefit of Machine Learning is its ability to detect anomalies and potential risks in real-time. This is particularly valuable in industries such as finance and healthcare, where timely detection of fraudulent activities or abnormal patient conditions can save millions of dollars and even lives.

However, to fully harness the power of Machine Learning, business leaders must invest in proper infrastructure and talent. This may involve hiring data scientists and investing in high-performance computing systems. Business leaders also need to ensure that their organizations have a strong data governance framework in place to ensure the security and privacy of sensitive information.

Furthermore, business leaders must be aware of potential biases in Machine Learning algorithms and work towards creating fair and ethical systems. This involves diverse and inclusive training data sets, as well as continuous monitoring and auditing of the algorithms to identify and address any potential biases.

CONCLUSION

In an age where digital transformation isn't just a buzzword, but a quintessential pathway to growth, generative artificial intelligence (generative AI) has emerged as a powerful tool. Before this term triggers images of science fiction or complex algorithms out of reach for small businesses, envisage creating art, designing websites, or generating leads with a touch of a button. Small businesses, listen up – this technology is no longer just for the big players; it's for anyone who wants to future-proof their business

At essence, generative AI refers to AI systems that create new data instances that resemble the 'training data'. It does this by assessing and mimicking patterns, often with startling accuracy. But how does this apply to small businesses, and why should it matter?

Generative AI has a wide spectrum of applications, from the artistic capabilities used for creating visual content to the more practical domains like natural language processing (NLP). For example, it can draft personalized responses to customer feedback, generate product design prototypes, and even compose ad content. The technology stands at the intersection of creativity and productivity, enabling businesses to automate tasks that previously required a human touch, thus freeing time.

Benefits For Small Business Owners

The versatility of generative AI means it can benefit small businesses across different spectrums. Here's how:

Enhanced Customer Experience

AI tools like chatbots that incorporate generative AI offer a more human-like interaction to customers, enhancing the user experience. These smart bots can hold natural conversations, answer detailed questions, and provide immediate support, all leading to better customer satisfaction and retention.

By automating repetitive tasks, generative AI can significantly reduce the workload on businesses with lean teams. This could include writing reports, scheduling meetings, or generating invoices, allowing employees to focus on more strategic initiatives.

Generative AI can analyze consumer data to create highly personalized marketing content at scale. Whether it's tailored emails, social media posts, or digital ads, this technology can optimize the marketing message to increase engagement and conversion rates.

Analytics is a core pillar for decision-making. Generative AI streamlines this by presenting information in easily digestible forms, and it can also predict future trends based on past data, aiding in more informed business strategies.

Challenges And Considerations

While the benefits are evident, small businesses must approach the integration of generative AI with caution. Some pertinent challenges include:

The initial financial investment for AI development or subscription to a service provider can be substantial. Small businesses need to carefully consider the return on investment (ROI) and long-term costs.

Data Security And Privacy

The use of generative AI necessitates significant volumes of data, often sensitive customer data. Ensuring robust security measures is vital to protect against breaches and maintain customer trust.

Training And Skill Development

Employee training is essential. Integrating generative AI requires a learning curve for the team, both in terms of understanding how to use the technology and in adapting to the changes it brings to their roles.

Case Studies

To demystify the role of generative AI in small businesses, case studies provide an insightful look into how it can be a successful driver for growth. We will explore stories where businesses with limited resources leveraged generative AI to achieve remarkable results.

The Personal Touch In E-commerce

Consider a boutique e-commerce store that uses generative AI to compose personalized product descriptions and customer emails. This level of individual attention and detail helped increase their customer retention by 30% in the first year of use.

Dynamic Content In Media

A local media outlet integrated generative AI to update website content dynamically based on reader preferences and online behavior. This resulted in a 40% increase in page views and a 25% increase in the time spent by readers on their site.

Future Outlook

The future for generative AI is exciting for small business owners. While the technology is already impressive, its capabilities are continuously expanding. With OpenAI's GPT-3 and similar models — which can handle complex language tasks — the potential for natural and hyper-personalized customer interactions has been taken to new heights.

Additionally, the democratization of AI technology means more accessible tools for small businesses to leverage. Keeping an eye on these developments and an open mind towards its integration can unlock innovative solutions for common entrepreneurial challenges.

MAY I ASK YOU FOR A SMALL FAVOR?

Before you go, please I need your assistance! In case you like this book, might you be able to please share your opinion on Amazon and compose a legit review? It will take only one moment for you, yet be an extraordinary favour for me. Since I'm not a famous writer and I don't have a large distributing organization supporting me. I read each and every review and hop around with happiness like a little child each time my audience remarks on my books and gives me their fair criticism! ☺. In case you didn't appreciate the book or had an issue with it, kindly get in touch with me via email Elio Scott@gmail.com and reveal to me how I can improve it.

Made in the USA
Las Vegas, NV
21 March 2025